The Complete Ethical Hacking Book

OrangeBooks Publication

Smriti Nagar, Bhilai, Chhattisgarh - 490020

Website:**www.orangebooks.in**

© Copyright, 2022, Author

All rights reserved. No part of this book may be reproduced, stored in a retrieval system, or transmitted, in any form by any means, electronic, mechanical, magnetic, optical, chemical, manual, photocopying, recording or otherwise, without the prior written consent of its writer.

First Edition, 2022

The Complete Ethical Hacking Book

Thirumalesh

OrangeBooks Publication
www.orangebooks.in

Legal Disclaimer

Any proceedings and or activities related to the material contained within this book are exclusively your liability. The misuse and mistreat of the information in this book can consequence in unlawful charges brought against the persons in question. The authors and review analyzers will not be held responsible in the event any unlawful charges brought against any individuals by misusing the information in this book to break the law. This book contains material and resources that can be potentially destructive or dangerous. If you do not fully comprehend something on this book, don't study this book. Please refer to the laws and acts of your state/region/ province/zone/territory or country before accessing, using, or in any other way utilizing these resources. These materials and resources are for educational and research purposes only. Do not attempt to violate the law with anything enclosed here within. If this is your intention, then leave now.

While using this book you agree to follow the below mentioned terms and conditions:

1. All the information provided in this book is for educational purposes only. The book author is no way responsible for any misuse of the information.

2. "The Complete Ethical Hacking Book" is just a term that represents the name of the book and is not a book that provides any illegal information. "The Complete Ethical Hacking Book" is a book related to Computer Security and not a book that promotes hacking/cracking/software piracy.

3. This book is totally meant for providing information on "Computer Security", "Network Security", "Web Application Secuirty" and other related topics and is no way related towards the terms "CRACKING" or "HACKING" (Unethical).

4. Few articles (tutorials) in this book may contain the information related to "Hacking Passwords", "Hacking Systems", "Hacking Websites" or "Hacking Email Accounts" (Or Similar terms). These are not the GUIDES of Hacking. They only provide information about the legal ways of retrieving the passwords. You shall not misuse the information to gain unauthorized access. However you may try out these hacks on your own computer at your own risk. Performing hack attempts (without permission) on computers that you do not own is illegal.

5. All the information in this book is meant for developing Hacker Defense attitude among the readers and help preventing the hack attacks. "The Complete Ethical Hacking Book" insists that this information shall not be used for causing any kind of damage directly or indirectly. However you may try these codes on your own computer at your own risk.

6. The word "Hack" or "Hacking" that is used in this book shall be regarded as "Ethical Hack" or "Ethical Hacking" respectively.

7. We believe only in White Hat Hacking. On the other hand we condemn Black Hat Hacking.

8. Most of the information provided in this book are simple computer tricks (may be called by the name hacks) and are no way related to the term hacking.

9. Some of the tricks provided by us may no longer work due to fixture in the bugs that enabled the exploits. We are not responsible for any direct or indirect damage caused due to the usage of the hacks provided in the book.

Preface

Computer hacking is the practice of altering computer hardware and software to carry out a goal outside of the creator's original intention. People who slot in computer hacking actions and activities are often entitled as hackers.

The majority of people assume that hackers are computer criminals. They fall short to identify the fact that criminals and hackers are two entirely unrelated things. Media is liable for this. Hackers in realism are good and extremely intelligent people, who by using their knowledge in a constructive mode help organizations, companies, government, etc. to secure credentials and secret information on the Internet.

Years ago, no one had to worry about Crackers breaking into their computer and installing Trojan viruses, or using your computer to send attacks against others. Now that thing have changed, it's best to be aware of how to defend your computer from damaging intrusions and prevent black hat hackers. Rampant hacking is systematically victimizing computers around the world. This hacking is not only common, but is being executed without a flaw that the attackers compromise a system, steal everything of value and entirely rub out their pathway within 20 minutes. So, in this Book you will uncover the finest ways to defend your computer systems from the hackers.

This Book is written by keeping one object in mind that a beginner, who is not much familiar regarding computer hacking, can easily, attempts these hacks and recognize what we are trying to demonstrate. Here we have incorporated the best ethical hacking articles in this volume, covering every characteristic linked to computer security.

After Reading this book you will come to recognize that how Hacking is affecting our every day routine work and can be very hazardous in many fields like bank account hacking etc. Moreover, after carrying out this book in detail you will be capable of understanding that how a hacker hacks and how you can defend yourself from these threats.

So Take care of yourself and Defend Yourself By hacking the hacker and be safe after that. So If you know how to hack a hacker then you can know how to prevent the hacker.

"Hack It and Have It..."
Thirumalesh(author)

Acknowledgements

Book or volume "The Complete Ethical Hacking Book" is tremendously complex to write, particularly without support of the Almighty GOD.

I thankful to my wife that what I can say that would justify or somehow verbalize what you mean to me? There is no doubt that this book is as much an effort on your part as mine. You gave me the wings of encouragement to fly and the dedication of long lonely days and nights while I worked on it. You never complained, never resisted, and were never upset when I needed more from you. Every man should be so lucky. I am who I am because of you. Thank you.

I say sorry and thankful to my little children you are the light of my life! I apologize for all early mornings, late nights, and long weekends on my work.

I also thankful to my mother and father for the gift of education and teaching me to understand the value of hard work and dedication to a project.

To finish, I am thankful to you also as you are reading this book. I am sure this book will make creative and constructive role to build your life more secure and alert than ever before.

- Thirumalesh

Index

Introduction To Hacking Environment 1
- Hacking 1
- Ethical Hacking 1
- Hacker 1
- Ethical Hacker 1
- Types Of Hackers 1
- Types Of Hacking: 2
- Why Ethical Hacking Is Necessary 2
- Steps To Perform Ethical Hacking 3
- Terminology 3
- What Is Information Security 4
- Famouse And Well Known Hackers: 4

Kali Linux 6
- Requirements To Run Kali Linux On The Host Machine 7

Google Hacking 8
- Google Advanced Operators: 8
- List Of Google Advanced Operators: 9
- Operator Syntax: 9
- Examples Of Valid Queries That Use Advanced Operators Include These: ... 10

Network Basics 13
- What Is Networking 13
- Network Components And Functions 13
- Types Of Networks 14
- OSI Model 14
- IP Address 16
- IP Address Classes 17
- Subnetwork (Subnet) 17
- Super Network (Supernet) 17

Network Address Translation 18
What Is DHCP, TCP, UDP, ICMP 18
Address Resolution Protocol 19
Domain Name System 19
Internet Group Management Protocol 19
Routing 19
Routing Protocol 19

Footprinting And Reconnaissance 21

Why Perform Footprinting 21
Terminology 21
What Kind Of Information Is Needed 22
How To Perform Footprinting 22
Google Hacking 22
Whois Lookup 23
Traceroute 23
IP Tracing 23
What If We Skip Footprinting? 23
Countermeasures 24

Scanning Networks 25

Scanning 25
Types Of Scanning 25
Network Scanning 26
List Of Network Scanners 26
What Are Ports And Port Numbers 26
Port Scanning 26
List Of Port Scanners 26
Few Well-Known Ports 27
ICMP 27
Live Host Identification Scan 27
TCP 27
UDP 27
TCP 3-Way Handshake 28
Tcp Communication Flags 28
TCP Connect Scan / Full Open Scan 28
SYN Scan / Half-Open Scan / Stealth Scan 29

ACK Scan/Firewall Detection 29
XMAS Scan 30
FIN Scan 30
NULL Scan 30
Importance Of Scanning 31

Enumeration 32

Enumeration 32
Netbios Enumeration 32
SMB Enumeration 33
DNS Enumeration 34
DNS - Domain Name Servers 34
DNS Records 34
DNS Record Types And Their Uses 34
DNS Zone Transfer 35
NTP Enumeration 35
SNMP Enumeration 35
SMTP Enumeration 35
Countermeasures 36

Vulnerability Analysis 37

Vulnerability 37
Vulnerability Research 37
Vulnerability Analysis 37
Objectives 38
Common Types Of Vulnerabilities 38
List Of Network Vulnerability Scanners 38
Types Of Vulnerability Assessment Reports 39
CVE (Common Vulnerabilities And Exposures) 39
CVSS (Common Vulnerability Scoring System) 39

System Hacking 40

System Hacking 40
Metasploit 40
Exploit 40
Payload 41

- Types Of Payload ... 41
- Shellcode ... 42
- Module ... 42
- Listener ... 42
- Escalating Privileges ... 42
- Vertical Privilege Escalation ... 42
- Horizontal Privilege Escalation ... 43
- Password Cracking ... 43
- Methods To Crack Password ... 43
- Countermeasures ... 44

Malware Threats ... 45

- Types Of Malware ... 45
- Trojan ... 45
- Symptoms Of Trojan Attack ... 45
- Trojan Detection ... 46
- Virus ... 46
- Worms ... 46
- Rootkit ... 47
- Spyware ... 47
- Ransomware ... 47
- Adware ... 47
- Backdoor ... 47
- Countermeasures ... 47

Sniffing ... 48

- Sniffer ... 48
- Types Of Sniffing ... 48
- Active Sniffing ... 48
- Passive Sniffing ... 49
- Protocols Vulnerable To Sniffing ... 49
- Port Mirroring (SPAN Port) ... 49
- Address Resolution Protocol ... 49
- ARP Spoofing ... 50
- DNS Spoofing ... 50
- Man In The Middle Attack ... 50
- Sniffing Detection Methods ... 51

Social Engineering 52

Social Engineering 52
Types Of Social Engineering 52
Human-Based 52
Computer Based 52
Mobile Based 53
Exploiting Human Using Social Engineering 53
Eavesdropping 54
Dumpster Diving 54
Shoulder Surfing 54
Tailgating And Piggybacking 54
Phishing 54
Spear Phishing 54
Countermeasures 55

Dos And Ddos Attack 56

Denial Of Service 56
Distributed Denial Of Service 56
Botnet 56
Exploiting System And Application Level Vulnerabilities 57
TCP SYN Flood 57
UDP Flood 58
HTTP Flood 59
Ping Of Death 59
MAC Flooding 59
Other Types Of Flooding 59

Session Hijacking 60

Session Token 60
Cookie 60
Attack Methods 61
Session Sniffing 61
Session Hijacking 61
Countermeasures From A General User Point Of View 62
Countermeasures From Web Developer Point Of View 62

Firewalls, Honeypots, IDS & IPS ... 63
Types Of Firewalls ... 63
Packet Filter Firewalls ... 63
Circuit-Level Gateways ... 64
Application-Level Gateways ... 64
Stateful Inspection Firewalls ... 64
Types Of Firewall Architectures ... 64
Bastion Host ... 64
Screened Subnet (DMZ) ... 65
Dual-Homed Firewall ... 65
List Of Firewall Products ... 66
Honeypot ... 66
Low Interaction Honeypot ... 66
High Interaction Honeypot ... 67
List Of Honeypots ... 67
Service Honeypots ... 67
Intrusion Detection System (IDS) ... 68
IDS Detection Methods ... 69
Types Of IDS ... 69
Network-Based IDS ... 69
Host-Based IDS ... 70
List Of Intrusion Detection Systems ... 70
Intrusion Prevention System (IPS) ... 71
Types Of IPS ... 71
Network-Based Intrusion Prevention Systems ... 71

Hacking Web Servers ... 73
Web Server ... 73
How Web Servers Work? ... 73
List Of Popular Web Servers ... 74
Footprinting Web Server ... 74
Web Server Vulnerabilities ... 74
Types Of Attacks Possible Against Web Servers ... 75
Impact Of Web Server Attacks ... 75
Identify Vulnerabilities On Web Server ... 76

Hacking Web Applications 77

Web Application 77
Types Of Websites 77
How A Web Application Works 77
OWASP 78
OWASP Top 10 Web Application Security Risks (2021)...................................... 78
Parameter Tampering 81
Directory Traversal 81
Cross-Site Request Forgery 81
Command Injection 81
File Inclusion 82
SQL Injection: 82
List Of Database Software 82
Database 82
SQL Injection 83
Authentication Bypass Attack 83
Error-Based SQL Injection 84
Blind SQL Injection 84
Countermeasures For SQL Injection Vulnerabilties 85
Countermeasures For Other Web Application Vulnerabilities 85

Hacking Mobile Platforms 86

Mobile Operating System 86
Mobile Platform Vulnerabilities And Risks 87
Android OS 87
Android Architecture 87
Iphone OS (IOS) 87
Ios Architecture 87
Hacking Android Device 88
General Guidelines For Mobile Security 88

Wireless Network Hacking (Wifi) 89

Wifi 89
WEP 89
WPA 89
WPA2 90

WPA3 90
  WPA3-Personal 91
  WPA3-Enterprise 91
  Types Of Wireless Antennas 92
  Aircrack-Ng 93
  Airmon-Ng 93
  Airodump-Ng 93
  Terminology: 93
  Aireplay-Ng 94
  Airbase-Ng 94
  WEP Cracking 94
  Cracking WPA/WPA2 Encryptionc 95
  Cracking The WPA Key Using A Wordlist 95
  Exploiting WPS Feature 95

Cloud Computing 97
  Cloud Computing 97
  Characteristics Of Cloud Computing 97
  Cloud Computing Services 98
  Cloud Deployment Models: 99
  Cloud Computing Benefits: 100
  Cloud Computing Threats 101
  Cloud Security Tools: 101

Cryptography 103
  Cryptography 103
  Objectives Of Cryptography 103
  Types Of Cryptography 104
  Cipher 105
  Classical Ciphers 105
  Modern Ciphers 106
  Hash Function 106
  Features Of Hash Functions 106
  Examples Of The Hash Functions 106
  Steganography 107
  Cryptography Attacks 107

1
Introduction To Hacking Environment

Hacking

Hacking is the process of exploiting system vulnerabilities and compromising security systems to gain unauthorized access to the system resources. It involves modifying system or application features to achieve a goal outside of the creator's original purpose.

Ethical Hacking

Ethical Hacking is the process to identify vulnerabilities to assure system security by use of hacking tools, tricks, and techniques. It focuses on simulating methods used by attackers to verify the existence of exploitable vulnerabilities in the system's security.

Hacker

Hackers are intelligent individuals who spend enormous amounts of time exploring computing resources like networks, websites, mobile devices, etc.

Ethical Hacker

Ethical Hacker is an expert in computer internals and networking concepts, who tries to find out potential vulnerabilities on the target systems before a hacker could use, without actually doing any harm to the information systems on behalf of the owners of the IT Assets.

Types of Hackers

1. **Black Hat (Crackers):** Individuals utilize computing skills for malicious or destructive activities.
2. **White Hat:** Individuals utilizing hacking skills for the defensive purpose
3. **Gray Hat:** Individuals who work both offensively and defensively

4. **Suicide Hackers:** Hackers who aim to shut down the critical infrastructure for a cause and are not worried about facing punishment.
5. **Script Kiddies:** An unskilled hacker who compromises the system by running scripts, tools, and software developed by real hackers.
6. **Cyber Terrorists:** Individuals with hacking skills, motivated by religious or political beliefs to create fear by large-scale disruption of computer networks.
7. **Hacktivist:** Hackers who promote a political agenda by hacking, especially by defacing or disabling websites.
8. **Government Sponsored:** Individuals employed by the government to penetrate and gain confidential information.

Types of Hacking:

- **Ethical Hacking:** Ethical hacking involves finding weaknesses in a computer or network system for testing purpose and finally getting them fixed.
- **Computer Hacking:** This is the process of stealing computer ID and password by applying hacking methods and getting unauthorized access to a computer system.
- **Website Hacking:** Hacking a website means taking unauthorized control over a web server and its associated software such as databases and other interfaces.
- **Password Hacking:** This is the process of recovering secret passwords from data that has been stored in or transmitted by a computer system.
- **Network Hacking:** Hacking a network means gathering information about a network by using tools like Nmap, Nessus, Openvas, Enumeration tools which are available in kali linux operating system etc. with the intent to harm the network system and hamper its operation.
- **Email Hacking:** It includes getting unauthorized access on an Email account and using it without taking the consent of its owner.

Why Ethical Hacking is Necessary

Ethical Hacker needs to think like malicious Hacker. Ethical hacking is necessary to defend against malicious hackers attempts, by anticipating methods they can use to break into a system.

- To fight against cyber crimes.
- To protect information from getting into wrong hands.
- To build a defensive mechanism that avoids hackers from penetrating.
- To test the organization's infrastructure security.

Steps to Perform Ethical Hacking

1. **Reconnaissance** refers to the pre-attack phase where an attacker observes a target before An attack. It may include the target organization's clients, employees, operations, network, and systems.

2. **Scanning** is the phase immediately preceding the attack. Here, the attacker uses the details gathered during reconnaissance to identify specific vulnerabilities. An attacker can gather critical network information such as the mapping of systems, routers, and firewalls by using simple tools such as the standard Windows utility Traceroute.

3. **Gaining Access** In this phase in which real hacking occurs. Attackers use vulnerabilities identified during the reconnaissance and scanning phase to gain access to the target system or network. Attackers gain access to the target system locally, over a LAN, or over the Internet.

4. **Maintaining Access** of the target machine and remain undetected. Attackers install a backdoor or a Trojan to gain repeat access. They can also install rootkits at the kernel level to gain full administrative access to the target computer. Rootkits are used to gain access at the operating system level, while a Trojan horse gains access at the application level. Both rootkits and Trojans require users to install them locally.

5. **Clearing Tracks** is for avoiding legal trouble, attackers will overwrite the server, System and application logs to Avoid suspicion and erase all evidence of their actions. Attackers can execute scripts in the Trojan or rootkit to replace the critical system and log files to hide their presence in the system.

Terminology

Vulnerability: In simple words, vulnerability is a loophole, Limitation, or weakness that becomes a source for an attacker to enter into the system.

Exploit: It is a software tool designed to take advantage of a aw (vulnerability) in a system for malicious purposes.

Payload: A payload is an action, or set of operations has to be done on the target, once the exploit successfully launched. It can be any control or Denial of service, etc.

Hack value: Hack value is a notion among the hackers that something is worth doing. Hackers may feel that breaking down robust network security might give them great satisfaction and that it is something they accomplished that not everyone could do.

Zero-day attack: In a 0-day attack, the attacker exploits the vulnerability before the software developer releases the Patch For them.

What is Information Security

Information security, sometimes shortened to InfoSec, is the practice of preventing unauthorized access, disclosure, disruption, destruction, modification, inspection, recording or destruction of information. Information security's primary focus is the balanced protection of the confidentiality, integrity, and availability of data and focuses on efficient policy implementation, organization productivity.

Famouse and well known Hackers:

1. **Kevin David Mitnick:** Is an American computer security consultant, author, and convicted hacker. He is best known for his high-profile 1995 arrested and five years in the prison for various computer and communications-related crimes.

   He is the first hacker to have his face immortalized on an FBI "Most Wanted" poster. He was formerly the most wanted computer criminal in the history of United States.

2. **Andrian Alfonso Lamo Atwood:** He was an American threat analyst and hacker. Lamo first gained media attention for breaking into several high-profile computer networks, including those of The New York Times, Yahoo, and Microsoft, culminating in his 2003 arrest.

   Lamo was best known for reporting U.S. soldier Chelsea Manning to Army criminal investigators in 2010 for leaking hundreds of thousands of sensitive U.S. government documents to WikiLeaks. Lamo died on March 14, 2018 at the age of 37.

3. **Jonathan Joseph James:** He is a Gray Hat Ethical Hacker and he was an American hacker who was the first juvenile incarcerated for cybercrime in the United States.

   In 1999 at the age of 16, he gained access to several computer's by breaking the password of a server that belonged to NASA and stole the source code of the International Space Station among other sensitive information.

2

Kali Linux

Kali Linux is a Debian-based Linux distribution aimed at advanced Penetration Testing and Security Auditing. Kali Linux contains several hundred tools which are geared towards various information security tasks, such as Penetration Testing, Security research, Computer Forensics and Reverse Engineering. Kali Linux is developed, funded and maintained by Offensive Security, a leading information security training company.

Kali Linux was released on the 13th March 2013 as a complete, top-to-bottom rebuild of BackTrack Linux, adhering completely to Debian development standards.

- **More than 600 penetration testing tools included:** After reviewing every tool that was included in BackTrack, we eliminated a great number of tools that either simply did not work or which duplicated other tools that provided the same or similar functionality. Details on what's included are on the Kali Tools site.

- **Free (as in beer) and always will be:** Kali Linux, like BackTrack, is completely free of charge and always will be. You will never, ever have to pay for Kali Linux.

- **Open source Git tree:** We are committed to the open source development model and our development tree is available for all to see. All of the source code which goes into Kali Linux is available for anyone who wants to tweak or rebuild packages to suit their specific needs.

- **FHS compliant:** Kali adheres to the Filesystem Hierarchy Standard, allowing Linux users to easily locate binaries, support files, libraries, etc.

- **Wide-ranging wireless device support:** A regular sticking point with Linux distributions has been supported for wireless interfaces. We have built Kali Linux to support as many wireless devices as we possibly can, allowing it to run properly on a wide variety of hardware and making it compatible with numerous USB and other wireless devices.

Requirements to run Kali Linux on the Host machine

Hardware:
- Minimum 4/8/16 GB RAM
- AMD2016 Model / intel core i5/i7 processor
- Minimum 80 GB Hard disk
- Minimum 15 Mbps internet speed

Software
- Virtual box software
- Kali Linux virtual machine image file (.ova)
- Metasploitable 2 virtual machine
- Windows 7 Operating System
- Windows 10 Operating System

3

Google Hacking

Google hacking, also named Google Dorking, is a hacker technique that uses Google Search and other Google applications to find security holes in the configuration and computer code that website are using.

Google hacking involves using advanced operators in the Google search engine to locate specific errors of text within search results. Some of the more popular examples are finding specific versions of vulnerable Web applications. A search query with **(inurl:hacker , intitle:version, filetype:pdf, mp4 etc..)** would locate all web pages that have that particular text contained within them. It is normal for default installations of applications to include their running version in every page they serve.

Devices connected to the Internet can be found. A search string such as

inurl:"ViewerFrame?Mode=" will find public web cameras.

Another useful search is following **intitle:index.of** followed by search keyword. This can give a list of files on the servers. For example, **intitle:index.of mp4** will give all the MP3 files available on various types of servers.

You can use symbols or words in your search to make your search results more precise. Note:

- Google Search usually ignores punctuation that isn't part of a search operator.
- Don't put spaces between the symbol or word and your search term. A search for **site:mysite.com** will work, but site: **mysite.com (it won't work).**

Google Advanced Operators:

Beyond the basic searching techniques explored in the previous chapter, Google offers special terms known as advanced operators to help you perform more advanced queries. These operators used properly, can help you get to exactly the information you're looking for without spending too much time poring over page after page of search results. When advanced operators are not provided in a query, Google will locate your search terms in any area of the web page, including the title, the text, the Uniform Resource Locator (URL), or the like. We will take a look at the following advanced operators in this chapter:

List of Google Advanced Operators:

intitle, allintitle	inurl, allinurl
filetype	allintext
site	link
inanchor	daterange
cache	info
related	phonebook
rphonebook	bphonebook
author	group
msgit	insubject
stocks	define

Operator Syntax:

- There is no space between the operator, the colon, and the search term. Violating this syntax can produce undesired results and will keep Google form understanding what you are trying to do. In most cases, Google will treat a syntactically bad advanced operator as just another search term. For example, providing the advanced operator *intitle* without a following colon and search term will cause Goolge to return pages that contain the word *intitle*.

- The *search_term* portion of an operator search follows the syntax discussed in the previous chapter. For example, a search term can be a single word or a phrase surrounded by quotes. If you use a phrase, just make sure there are no spaces between the operator, the colon, and the first quote of the phrase.

- Boolean operators and special characters (such as OR and +) can still be applied to advanced operator queries, but be sure they don't get in the way of the separating colon.

- Advanced operators can be combined in a single query as long as you honor both the basic *Google* query syntax as well as the advanced operator syntax. Some advanced operators combine better than others, and some simply cannot be combined. We will take a look at these limitations later in this chapter.

Thirumalesh

- The ALL operators (the operators beginning with the word ALL) are oddballs. They are generally used once per query and cannot be mixed with other operators.

Examples of valid queries that use advanced operators include these:

- **Intitle:Google** – This query will return pages that have the word Google in their title.

- **Intitle:"index of"** – This query will return pages that have the phrase "*index of* " in their title. Remember from the previous chapter that this query could also be given as "intitle:index.of", since the period serves as any character. This technique also makes it easy to supply a phrase without having to type the spaces and the quotation marks around the phrase.

- **Intitle:"index of " private** – This query will return pages that have the phrase "*index of*" in their title and also have the word "private" anywhere in the page, including in the URL, the tile, the text, and so on. Notice that "intitle" only applies to the phrase "*index of*" and not the word "private" since the first unquoted space follows the phrase "*index of*". Google interprets that space as the end of your advanced operator search term and continues processing the rest of the query.

- **intitle: "index of" "backup files"** – This query will return pages that have the phrase "*index of*" in their title and the phrase "backup files" anywhere in the page, including the URL, the title the text, and so on. Again, notice that "intitle" only applies to the phrase "*index of*".

Example:
Inurl:"ViewerFrame?Mode=

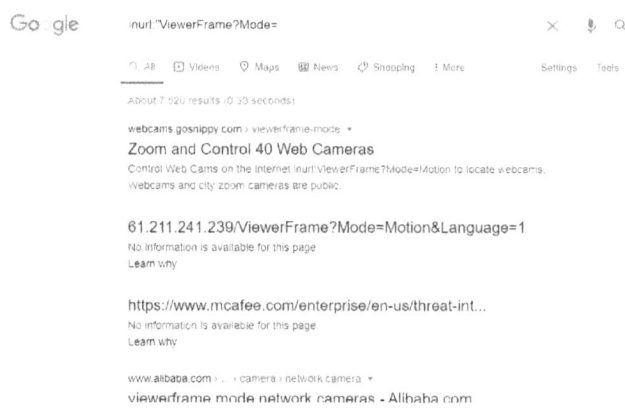

10

filetype:pdf hacking books

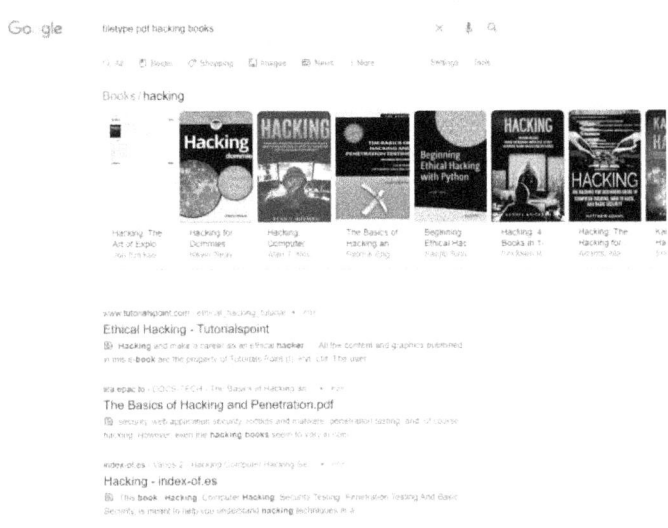

inurl:id=

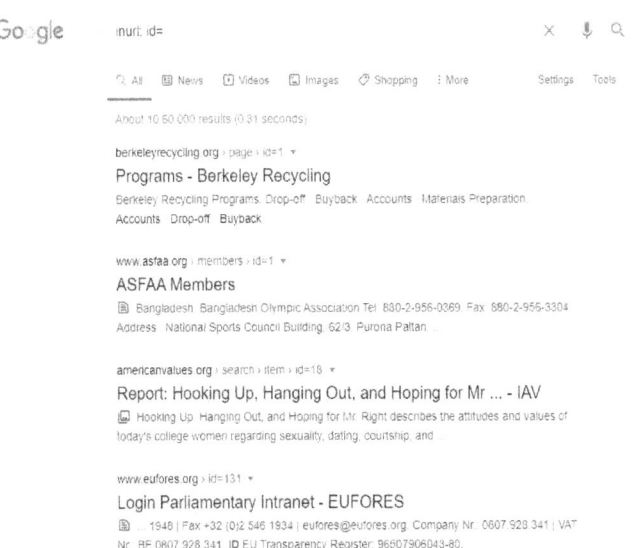

inurl:telugu mp4

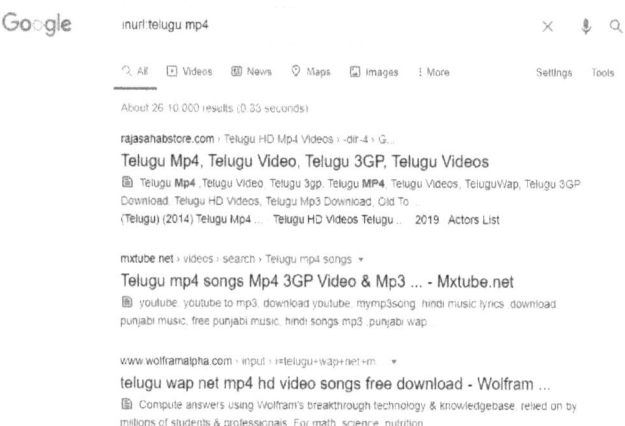

Hackers use Advanced Google Hacking methods to get the more information about the targeted industry, person or website with the help of advanced Google Hacking techniques.

The website called www.exploit-db.com have the option of Google Hacking Database(GHDB) is a compendium of Google hacking search terms that have been found to reveal sensitive data exposed by vulnerable servers and web applications. The GHDB was launched in 2000.

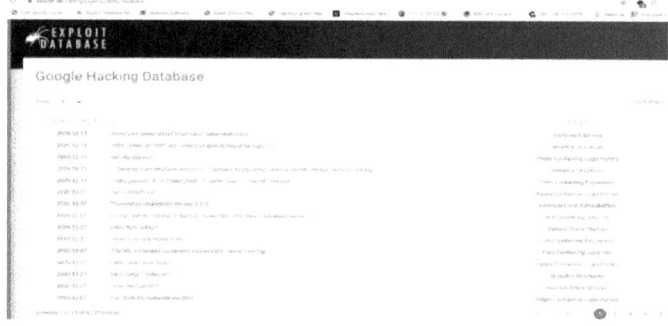

4

Network Basics

What is Networking

A network is a group of two or more computer systems or other devices that are linked together to exchange data. In networks, computing devices exchange data with each other using data links between nodes. These data links are established with the help of cable media such as wires or wireless media such as WiFi.

Network Components and Functions

Server: A computer or device on a network that manages network resources. Servers are often dedicated, meaning that they perform no other tasks besides their server tasks like accepts and responds to requests made by another program, known as a client.

Client: A client is an application that runs on a personal computer or workstation and relies on a server to perform some operations. The client accesses the server by way of a network.

Devices: Computer devices, such as a CD-ROM drive or printer, that is not part of the essential computer. Examples of devices include disk drives, printers, and modems.

Hub: Hub is a network hardware device for connecting multiple devices and making them act as a single network segment. A hub works at the physical layer of the OSI model.

Switch: A device that filters and forwards packets between LAN segments. Switches operate at the data link layer and sometimes the network layer of the OSI Reference Model.

Router: A router is a device that is capable of forwarding data packets on a network. Routers are placed at the junction (gateway) of two or more networks connect. Routers use headers and forwarding tables to determine the best path for forwarding the packets.

Bridge: Bridge is a computer networking device that connects a local area network (LAN) to another local area network that uses the same protocol.

Access Point: A hardware device or a computer's software that acts as a communication hub for users to connect all their wireless device.

Types of Networks

Local area network (LAN)
A LAN is a network that connects computers and devices in a limited geographical area such as a home, school, office building.

Wide area network (WAN)
A WAN is a computer network that covers a large geographic area such as a city, country, or spans even intercontinental distances. A WAN uses a communications channel that combines many types of media such as telephone lines, ethernet cables, optical fibers, etc.

Metropolitan Area Networks (MAN)
Metropolitan area Network covers a larger area than that of a LAN and smaller area when compared to WAN. MANs rarely extend beyond 100 KM and comprise a combination of different hardware and transmission media.

Wireless Local Area Network (WLAN)
Wireless local area networks provide wireless network communication over short distances using radio or infrared signals instead of traditional network cabling. WLANs are built by attaching a device called the access point to the edge of the wired network. Clients communicate with the AP using a wireless network adapter similar in function to a traditional Ethernet adapter.

Virtual private network (VPN)
The virtual private network is an overlay network in which some of the links between nodes are carried by virtual circuits in the network instead of physical wires. The data link layer protocols of the virtual network are said to be tunneled through the network. Personal Area Network (PAN)

A personal area network is a computer network organized around an individual. Personal area networks typically involve mobile devices. Personal area networks can be wired or wirelessly. These networks generally cover a network range of 10 meters (about 30 feet).

OSI model

OSI (Open Systems Interconnection) is a reference model for how applications communicate over a network. The main concept of OSI is that the process of communication between two endpoints in a network can be divided into seven distinct groups of related functions or layers. Each communicating user or program is on a device that can provide those seven layers of function. The seven Open Systems Interconnection layers are:

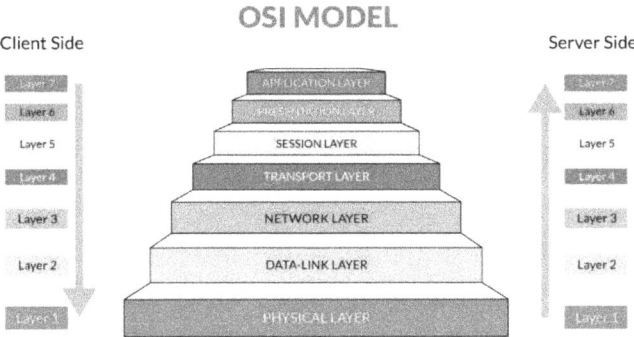

Layer 1: Physical Layer
This layer conveys the bit stream across the network either electrically, mechanically or through radio waves. The physical layer covers a variety of devices and mediums, among them cabling, connectors, receivers, transceivers, and repeaters.

Layer 2: Data Link Layer
This layer sets up links across the physical network, putting packets into network frames. This layer has two sublayers the logical link control layer and the media access control layer (MAC). MAC layer types include Ethernet and wireless specifications.

Layer 3: Network Layer
This layer handles addressing and routing the data. To transfer it from the right source to the right destination. The IP address is part of the network layer.

Layer 4: Transport Layer
This layer manages packetization of data, then the delivery of the packets, including checking for errors in the data once it arrives. On the internet, TCP and UDP provide these services for most applications.

Layer 5: Session Layer
The session layer controls the connections between computers. It establishes, manages and terminates the connections between the local and remote application.

Layer 6: Presentation Layer

This layer is usually part of an operating system (OS) and converts incoming and outgoing data from one presentation format to another for example, from clear text to encrypted text at one end and back to clear text at the other.

Layer 7: Application Layer

The application layer of the OSI model interacts with the end user. Protocols at this layer handle the requests from different software applications. If a web browser wants to download an image, an email client wants to check the server, and a file-sharing program wants to upload a movie, the protocols in the application layer will process those requests.

IP address

An Internet Protocol address (IP address) is a numerical label assigned to each device connected to a computer network. IP address serves two purposes, host or network interface identification and location addressing. Internet Protocol version 4 (IPv4) defines an IP address as a 32-bit number and new version of IP (IPv6), uses 128 bits for the IP address.

Private IP address: A private IP address is a non-Internet facing IP address. Private IP addresses are provided by network devices, such as routers, using network address translation (NAT).

Public IP address: A public IP address is an IP address that can be accessed over the Internet. The public IP address is a globally unique IP address assigned to a computing device.

IPv4: Internet Protocol Version 4 is the fourth revision of the Internet Protocol used to identify devices on a network. IPv4 is the most widely deployed Internet protocol used to connect devices to the Internet. IPv4 uses a 32-bit address scheme allowing a total of 2^32 addresses.

IPv6: Internet Protocol Version 6 is the newest version of the Internet Protocol reviewed in the IETF standards committees to replace the current version of IPv4. IPv6 addresses are 128-bit IP address written in hexadecimal and separated by colons. An example IPv6 address could be written like this 3ffe: 1900:4545:3:200: f8ff: fe21:67cf.

IP address classes

There are five classes of IP addresses, they are Class A, Class B, Class C, Class D and Class E, where only A, B, and C are commonly used.

Class	Address Range	Supports
Class A	1.0.0.1 to 126.255.255.254	Supports 16 million hosts on each of 127 networks.
Class B	128.1.0.1 to 191.255.255.254	Supports 65,000 hosts on each of 16,000 networks.
Class C	192.0.1.1 to 223.255.254.254	Supports 254 hosts on each of 2 million networks.
Class D	224.0.0.0 to 239.255.255.255	Reserved for multicast groups.
Class E	240.0.0.0 to 254.255.255.254	Reserved for future use, or Research and Development Purposes.

Subnetwork (Subnet)

A subnet is a logical subdivision of an IP network. Dividing a network into two or more networks is known as subnetting. Computers that belong to a subnet are addressed with a significant bit-group in their IP addresses. Subnetting results in the logical division of an IP address into two parts, the network address, and the host identifier.

Super network (Supernet)

Supernet is an Internet Protocol network that is formed, for combining two or more networks into a larger network. The benefits of supernetting are conservation of address space, gaining efficiency regarding memory storage and route information processing.

Network address translation

Network address translation (NAT) is a method of remapping one IP address space into another by modifying network address information in IP header packets while they are in transit. It has become a popular and essential tool in conserving global address space in the face of IPv4 address exhaustion.

What is DHCP, TCP, UDP, ICMP

Dynamic Host Configuration Protocol

The Dynamic Host Configuration Protocol (DHCP) is a network management protocol used on UDP/IP networks. A DHCP server dynamically assigns an IP address and other network configuration parameters to each device on a network so that they can communicate with other IP networks.

TCP
TCP stands for Transmission Control Protocol, which is a widely used protocol for data transmission over a network. TCP establishes a connection between two hosts before transmitting data, to ensure that data transmitted over the network reaches the destination without fail. TCP also known as a connection-oriented protocol, establishes a reliable connection between sender and receiver. TCP provides error and flow control mechanisms which help in orderly transmission of data and retransmission of lost packets.

UDP
UDP stands for User Datagram Protocol, which is connectionless protocol, mostly used for connections that can tolerate data loss. UDP is used by applications on the internet that offer voice and video communications, which can suffer some data loss without adversely affecting the quality. UDP does not provide error and flow control mechanisms because of which it does not require a connection to be established before transmitting data over the network.

ICMP
ICMP stands for Internet Control Message Protocol; this is widely used for internet communication troubleshooting or generated in response to errors in IP operations, this will send packets to the target machine and will see whether the packets are delivered or not.

Address Resolution Protocol

Address Resolution Protocol (ARP) is a communication protocol used for discovering the link layer address, such as a MAC address, associated with a given network layer address. This mapping is a critical function in the Internet Protocol suite. It works within the boundaries of a single network never routed across internetworking nodes. ARP uses a simple message format containing one address resolution request or response. The size of the ARP message depends on the link layer and network layer address sizes.

Domain Name System

Domain Name System (DNS) is a naming system for resources connected to the Internet or a private network. The DNS is responsible for assigning domain names and mapping those names to Internet resources by designating name servers for each domain. Network administrators have authority over the subdomains of their allocated namespace to other name servers. Domain Name System is an essential component of Internet functionality.

Internet Group Management Protocol

Internet Group Management Protocol (IGMP) is a communication protocol used by hosts and adjacent routers on IPv4 networks to establish multicast group memberships. IGMP is an integral part of IP multicast. IGMP can be used for one-to-many networking applications such as online video streaming and gaming and allows the more efficient use of resources.

Routing

Routing is the process of selecting a path for traffic in a network or across multiple networks. In routing, network packets from their source toward their destination are routed through intermediate network nodes by specific packet forwarding mechanisms. Intermediate nodes are typically networked hardware devices such as routers, bridges, gateways, firewalls, or switches. In routing, process packets are directed on based on routing tables, which maintain a record of the routes to various network destinations. An administrator specifies the routing table.

Routing protocol

Routing protocol specifies how routers communicate with each other, distributing information, which enables them to select routes between any two nodes on a computer network. Routing algorithms determine to choose a specific route. A routing protocol shares this information first among immediate neighbors, and then throughout the network. The major types of routing protocols.

- Routing Information Protocols (RIP)
- Interior Gateway Routing Protocol (IGRP)
- Open Shortest Path First (OSPF)
- Exterior Gateway Protocol (EGP)
- Enhanced Interior Gateway Routing Protocol (EIGRP)
- Border Gateway Protocol (BGP)
- Intermediate System-to-Intermediate System (IS-IS).

5

Footprinting And Reconnaissance

Footprinting is the process of collecting information related to the target network.

Footprinting helps in identifying Various ways to intrude into an Organization's network system.

In this step attacker tries to gather publicly available sensitive information, using which he/she can carry out social engineering, perform system or network level attacks, that can cause substantial financial loss or damage the reputation of an individual or organization. This step helps an attacker in gaining a basic idea of network structure and organization's infrastructure details.

Why perform Footprinting

- Footprinting is the first step of the attacking process. Hackers use to gather information about the target environment, usually to find ways to break into that environment.
- Footprinting allows an attacker to know about the security posture of an organization.
- It helps in reducing attacker's attack surface to a specific range of IP address, networks, domain name, remote access, etc.
- It allows an attacker to build their information database about the target's organization security weakness and plan attacks accordingly.

Terminology

Passive Information Gathering: Is the process of collecting information about the target from the publicly accessible resources.

Active Information Gathering: Is the process of gather information about the target by using techniques likes social engineering, grabbing information by visiting personal blogs or websites, or through direct interaction with the individual or employees of the organization.

What kind of information is needed

Network Information:
Domain name, Network blocks, IP address of computers in the target network, TCP and UDP services running, details related to IDS running.

System Information:
User and group names, system banners, routing tables information, system architecture, remote system names.

Organization Information:
Employee details, organization website details, location details, address and phone numbers, information related to security policies implemented, and any non-technical information about the organization

How to perform Footprinting

- Through search engines
- Through social networking sites
- Through official websites
- Direct communication with the target
- Through job portals
- Through DNS enumeration

Google Hacking

Google is a vast resource where millions of pages are available for an average user to search. But getting useful information out of those results is a challenging task, to extract the desired information (information that is useful to attack target individual or network) we can take help of Google search operators also known as google dorks. This technique is called Google Hacking.

By using these google dorks, we query Google to reveal sensitive data, useful for the reconnaissance stage of an attack, sensitive data such as emails associated with an individual or an organization, database files with usernames and passwords, unprotected directories with confidential documents, URLs to login portals, different types of system logs such as firewall and access logs etc.,

Whois Lookup

While purchasing a domain, the user (registrant) has to provide their contact details, like address, phone number, email id, etc., those registration details along with domain validity information is usually stored in a publicly available database called whois database.

Domain registrars will protect this information from not to be published on the internet based on the request made by users, at extra cost. Domain registration details will not be available on the internet if they opt domain privacy, of course, domain registrar information will be available, whoever wants to get that domain information should contact the registrar, and if the registrar finds the query is legitimate, they will provide the Domain registrant details. By using the free online and offline tools, we extract domain registrant Information from publicly available Whois database. This process is known as whois lookup.

Traceroute

While the data packet is in transit, it passes through multiple network nodes to reach the destination. If the data packet fails to reach the destination, the user will not know the reason behind the failure; network administrators use traceroute program to trace the packet from source to destination to identify the actual cause of the problem so that they can investigate and resolve the issue.

Traceroute tool is used to extract details about the path that a packet takes from the source to a specific destination.

IP Tracing

The IP address is one of the most critical pieces of information. To attack the target computer, attackers need to identify the IP address of the target computer. Attackers use different techniques to grab the IP address. Sending tracking emails, or SMS, or some malicious links to grab the IP address of the target computer is called as IP Tracing. In other words, extracting user details (like location) based on IP address is known as IP Tracing or IP Lookup.

What if We Skip Footprinting?

We should not skip Footprinting. Hacker or penetration tester's success will not always depend on sophisticated tools used to perform attacks, but information gathered at Footprinting plays a crucial role in gaining access to the target. Want to know how?

Scenario: Information gathered in this step can help us bypass some security controls for example login credentials for one of the computers in the network may be DOB or first name of the employee. As we know some necessary information about an employee, we can try to guess the username or password by observing hint.

Conclusion: launching attacks without proper knowledge about the target may affect the success of the attack.

Countermeasures

- Revise the information before publishing on blogs, social networking sites, and websites.
- Never upload highly classified documents online.
- Privatize the who is lookup registration details by applying for anonymous registration with the web hosting service provider.
- Never click the link in emails or mobiles, if received from an unknown sender.
- Use pseudo-names in blogs and social networking sites to not leak personal information.
- Avoid opening third-party social networking sites or websites from office premises.
- Use IDS in corporate networks to detect Footprinting attacks done by hackers.

6

Scanning Networks

Scanning

Scanning is a process of identifying network and service related information by communicating with the target. Scanning helps in identifying IP/Hostnames, Ports, Services running on ports, Live hosts, Vulnerable services running on the target network.

Types of Scanning

Network Scanning – Identifying the number of computers on the network.

- Ping Sweep
- Arp Scan

Port Scanning – Listing open ports and services running on those ports.

- SYN Scan/Stealth Scan/Half-Open Scan
- TCP Connect Scan
- ACK Scan/Firewall Detection Scan
- XMAS Scan
- FIN Scan
- NULL Scan
- OS Detection Scan
- Script Scan
- UDP Scan
- Service Detection Scan

Network Scanning

During the network scanning process, attackers gather a list of IP addresses of computers that are live on the target network. The job of the attacker will be easy if he/she can analyze the network structure and services running on each machine.

List of Network Scanners

- Angry IP Scanner
- Advanced IP Scanner
- Netdiscover
- Autoscan
- hping3
- Nmap

What Are Ports and Port Numbers

Ports are virtual entry points to any digital device; devices can communicate with one to another using port, there are virtually 65535 ports available in every device, those can be identified with port numbers, ranging from 0 to 65535.

0	1023	Well known ports
1024	49135	Random ports
49136	65535	Experimental ports

Port Scanning

Port scanning is a technique where the attacker will send communication probes to targets to see how the target is responding to them, based on the response attacker will determine what ports are open and several other port details, like service running on the port numbers, and OS the target is running.

List of Port scanners

- Nmap
- SuperScan
- Strobe
- Zenmap (Available for Windows Also)

Few Well-Known Ports

Application	Port Number(s)	Application	Port Number(s)
FTP	20–21	DNS	53
Telnet	23	IRC	194
SMTP	25	POP3	110
DNS	53	SNMP	161
HTTP	80	HTTPS	443
SSH	22	NetBIOS	139
TFTP	69	SQL	156

For details on other port numbers and services refer RFC-1700

ICMP

ICMP stands for Internet Control Messaging Protocol; this is widely used for internet communication troubleshooting or to generate errors related to IP operations, this will send packets to the target machine and will see whether the packets are delivered or not.

Live Host identification scan

Identifying the turned-on computers by sending ICMP packets or ARP packets or some other kind of packets is called Live Host Identification Scan.

TCP

Transmission Control Protocol (TCP), which is a widely used protocol for data transmission over a network. This protocol establishes a reliable connection between two hosts before transmitting data, to ensure that data transmitted over the network reaches the destination without fail. TCP also known as a connection-oriented protocol, establishes a reliable connection between sender and receiver. TCP provides error and flow control mechanisms which help in orderly transmission of data and retransmission of lost packets.

UDP

UDP stands for User Datagram Protocol, which is connectionless protocol, mostly used for connections that can tolerate data loss. UDP is used by applications on the internet that offer voice and video communications, which can suffer some data loss without adversely affecting the quality. UDP does not provide error and flow control mechanisms because of which it does not require a connection before transmitting data over the network.

TCP 3-way Handshake

To start a proper TCP conversation, the sender and receiver perform 3- way handshake before exchanging data over the network. It is a process used by two hosts to agree upon some protocol stack to start sharing data. Following image represents the process of 3-way handshake.

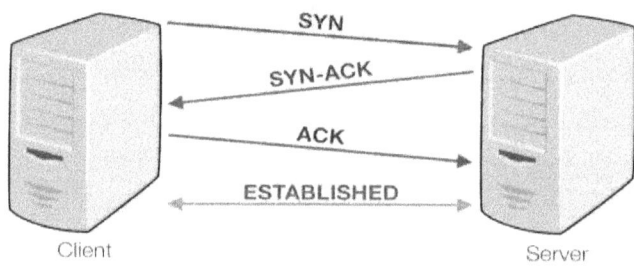

Tcp Communication Flags

1. **SYN (Synchronize):** SYN flags will be used to initiate a data transfer of the start of a communication process.

2. **ACK (Acknowledgement):** ACK flags will be used to send the receipt of successful packet transmission.

3. **FIN (Finish):** FIN flags will be used to close or finish an existed packet transmission. No more packets to be received.

4. **RST (Reset):** RST flags will be used to terminate or reset a connection.

5. **URG (Urgent):** Data in this flagged packet should   be processed immediately.

6. **PSH (Push):** Sends all buffered data immediately.

TCP Connect Scan / Full Open Scan

Nmap directly communicates with the operating system to establish a connection with the target machine and port by issuing the connect system call.

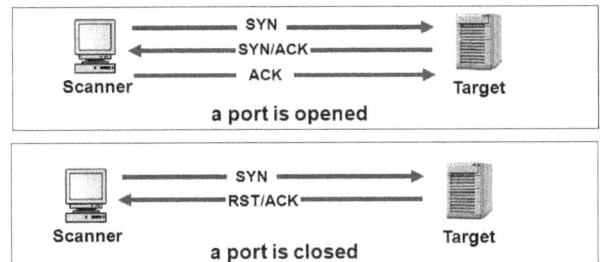

SYN Scan / Half-Open Scan / Stealth Scan

SYN scan is the most popular scan option. It can scan thousands of ports in a short period on a fast network not hampered by restrictive firewalls.

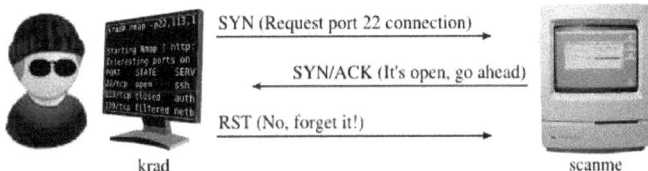

ACK Scan/Firewall Detection

This scan is different from others scanning operations discussed before; it never determines open ports. It is used to identify firewall rules, determining the type of firewall and identify filtered ports.

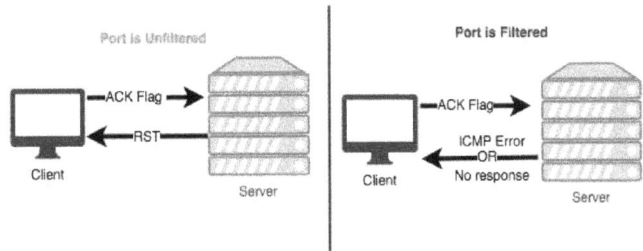

XMAS Scan

The Xmas- Tree scan sends a TCP packet with the following flags:

URG - Indicates that the data is urgent and should be processed immediately

PSH - Forces data to a buffer

FIN - Used when finishing a TCP session

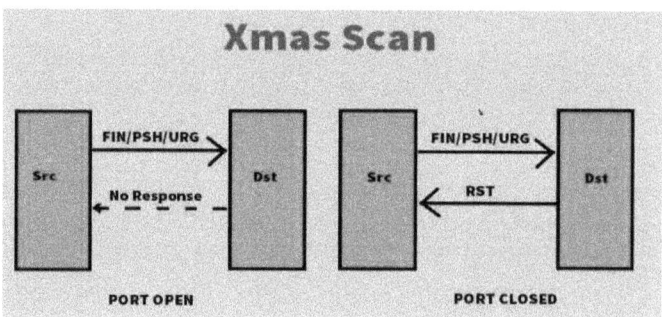

FIN Scan

FIN scan, which attempts to close a connection that isn't open. The operating system generates an error if service is not running on target port. If a service is listening, the operating system will silently drop the incoming packet. Therefore, no response indicates a listening service at the port.

NULL Scan

A data packet with zero flag values will be sent to a TCP port. (In a regular TCP communication, at least one bit or flag is set). In TCP connect / SYN scans, a response indicates an open port, but in a NULL scan, a response indicates a closed port.

Importance of Scanning

Scanning will provide an exact outline of the network structure of the target workspace. It is beneficial for hacking target servers or individual computers. Scanning will provide a blueprint of entire network and details about devices running on the network, information related to network topology and helps in deciding what operating system is running on target computers.

Countermeasures

- Block ICMP and UDP inbound.

- Disable unused ports with support of policy settings.

- Block internal IP addresses from coming inbound.

- Change system and application banners to counter software detection attacks.

- Always use a genuine operating system, update it frequently.

- Use IDS & IPS to detect and prevent attacks.

- Use "duckduckgo" or "StartPage" search engine to protect privacy.

7
Enumeration

Enumeration

Enumeration is the process of establishing an active connection to the target host to discover potential attack vectors in the computer system, information gained at this phase can be used for further exploitation of the system. It is often considered as a critical phase because few pieces of information gathered in this phase can help us directly exploit the target computer.

Information gathered in this phase
1. Usernames, Group names
2. Hostnames
3. Network shares and services
4. IPtables and routing tables
5. Service settings and Audit configurations
6. Application and banners
7. SNMP and DNS Details

NetBIOS enumeration

NetBIOS stands for Network Basic Input Output System. It allows computers to communicate over a LAN to share files and devices like printers. NetBIOS names are used to identify network devices over TCP/IP.

NetBIOS Name List:

Name	NetBIOS code	NetBIOS code	Information Obtained
<host name>	<00>	UNIQUE	Hostname
<domain>	<00>	GROUP	Domain name
<host name>	<03>	UNIQUE	Messenger service running for that computer
<user name>	<03>	UNIQUE	Messenger service running for that individual logged-in user
<host name>	<20>	UNIQUE	Server service running
<domain>	<1D>	GROUP	Master browser name for the subnet
<domain>	<1B>	UNIQUE	Domain master browser name, identifies the PDC for that domain

Benefits of NetBIOS Enumeration:

1. Information related to computers that belong to a domain.
2. Details related to shares on computers in the network.
3. Extracting policies and passwords.

SMB Enumeration

SMB stands for Server Message Block. It is mainly used for providing shared access to files, printers and miscellaneous communications between nodes on a network. It also provides an authenticated inter-process communication mechanism.

DNS Enumeration

DNS enumeration retrieves information regarding all the DNS servers and their corresponding records related to an organization. DNS enumeration will yield usernames, computer names, and IP addresses of potential target systems.

DNS - Domain Name Servers

The Internet equivalent of the phone book. They maintain the directory of domain names & translate them to internet protocol addresses.

DNS Records

The list of DNS records provides an overview of types of resource records stored in the zone files of the domain name system. The DNS implements a distributed, hierarchical and redundant database for information associated with internet domain names & addresses.

DNS record types and their uses

-A (Address) maps hostnames to IPv4 address.
-SOA (Start of Authority) identifies the DNS server responsible for the domain information.
-CNAME (Canonical Name) Provides additional names or aliases for the address.
-AAAA (Address) maps hostnames to IPv6 address.
-MX (Mail exchange) Identifies the mail server for the domain
-SRV (Service) Identifies services such as directory services
-PTR (Pointer) Maps IP address to hostnames
-NS (Nameserver) Identifies other name servers for the domain

DNS Zone Transfer

- Used to replicate DNS data across some DNS Servers or to backup DNS files. A user or server will perform a specific zone transfer request from a name server.

- DNS servers should not permit zone transfers towards any IP address from the Internet.

- Since zone files contain complete information about domain names, subdomains and IP addresses configured on the target name server, finding this information is useful for increasing your attack surface and for better understanding the internal structure of the target company.

- We can identify hidden subdomains, development servers information, and internal IP addresses, etc.

- Information gathered from zone files can be useful for attackers to implement various attacks against the target company, like targeting test or development servers which are less secure.

NTP Enumeration

NTP (Network Time Protocol) utilizes UDP port 123. Through NTP enumeration you can gather information such as a list of hosts connected to NTP server, IP addresses, system names, and operating systems running on the client system in a network. All this information can be enumerated by querying the server.

SNMP Enumeration

Simple Network Management Protocol is an application layer protocol which uses UDP protocol to maintain and manage routers, hubs, switches and other network devices. SNMP is a popular protocol found enabled on a variety of operating systems like Windows Server, Linux & UNIX servers as well as network devices.

SMTP Enumeration

SMTP enumeration allows us to determine valid users on the SMTP server.

With the help of built-in SMTP commands, we can gather useful information.

1. VRFY - Is used for validating users.
2. EXPN – Reveals the actual delivery address of mailing lists.
3. RCPT TO - It defines the recipients of the message.

Countermeasures

- Install IDS & IPS to detect and stop Enumerating attacks done on any ports.
- Install honeypot application in a proxy server to give false information to the hacker.
- Upload robots.txt file in the website to stop Footprinting of directories.
- Enable DNSSec option in server OS to avoid information leakage through DNS server.
- Hosts can be locked down and securely configured and patched. Limit services to only those needed.
- Network services can be locked down and made not to give up as much useful information to a hacker.
- Changing default security configuration is very important.
- Block ports to unknown hosts.
- Turn off file and print sharing services in windows.
- Prevent DNS zone transfers to unknown hosts.

8

Vulnerability Analysis

Vulnerability

A bug or flaw or a state of being exposed which leads to a critical hacking attack from the Hacker is called Vulnerability.

Vulnerability Research

It is the process by which security flaws in technology are identified. Vulnerability research does not always involve reverse engineering, code analysis, etc. Performing vulnerability research against technology pre-release enables technology vendors to provide their customers with higher quality products and higher levels of trust and security.

List of vulnerability research websites
- securityfocus.com
- vulnerability-lab.com
- us-cert.gov
- packetstormsecurity.com
- nvd.nist.gov
- cvedetails.com

Vulnerability Analysis

Vulnerability analysis is the process of defining, identifying, classifying and prioritizing vulnerabilities in computer systems, applications or network infrastructure. This phase allows the organization to perform security assessment with the necessary knowledge, awareness and risk background to understand the threats and react appropriately.

Attackers perform vulnerability analysis to identify security loopholes in the target organization's network or communication infrastructure. Attackers take advantage of identified vulnerabilities to perform further exploitation of that target network.

The vulnerability scanner (software) compares details about the target attack surface to a database of information about known security vulnerabilities in services and ports, anomalies in packet construction, and potential paths to exploitable programs or scripts.

Objectives

- Identify vulnerabilities ranging from critical design flaws to simple misconfigurations.
- Document the vulnerabilities so that the developers andnetworks administrators can easily identify and reproduce the findings.
- Create guidance to assist network administrators and developers with remediating the identified vulnerabilities

Common types of Vulnerabilities

- Missing data encryption
- SQL injection
- Buffer-overflow
- Missing authentication for critical functions
- Missing authorization
- Unrestricted upload of dangerous file types
- Cross-site request forgery
- Download of codes without integrity checks
- Weak passwords
- Path/Directory traversal

List of network vulnerability scanners

- Nessus
- GFI LanGuard - Scans both Hardware & Software Vulnerabilities.
- Qualys guard - Works both on LAN & WAN
- Saint
- Nexpose - Paid and free solution available from Offensive security
- Core impact - Scanner and Exploit framework

- OpenVAS

Types of Vulnerability Assessment Reports

- **Technical Report** - Includes detailed description related to vulnerabilities found on the target computer(s)

- **Non-Technical Report** - Brief report on vulnerabilities found on the target computer(s). This report includes graphs and charts that are easy to understand the risk.

CVE (Common Vulnerabilities and Exposures)

CVE is a dictionary of standardized identifiers for common software vulnerabilities and exposures. CVE IDs, i.e., CVE-2018-1002100 which are assigned by CVE Numbering Authorities from around the world, ensures confidence when used to share information about a unique software or firmware vulnerability, provides a baseline for tool evaluation, and enables data exchange. CVE IDs act as a benchmark for evaluating security services.

CVSS (Common Vulnerability Scoring System)

CVSS is a published standard that provides an open framework for communicating the characteristics and impacts of IT vulnerabilities. Its quantitative model ensures accurate measurement while enabling users to see the underlying vulnerability characteristics that were used to generate the scores. The National Vulnerability Database (NVD) provides CVSS scores for almost all known vulnerabilities. CVSS assessment consists of three metrics for measuring vulnerabilities

1. **Base Metrics:** It represents the inherent qualities of a vulnerability
2. **Temporal Metrics:** It represents the features that keep on changing during the lifetime of a vulnerability.
3. **Environmental Metrics:** It represents the vulnerabilities that are based on a particular environment or implementation.

Each metrics sets a score from 1-10, ten being the most severe. CVSS score is calculated and generated by a vector string, which represents the numerical score for each group in the form of a block of text. CVSS calculator is developed to rank the security vulnerabilities and provide the user with overall severity and risk related to the vulnerability.

9

System Hacking

System Hacking

System hacking is the process of trying to compromise the target system with the help of the information we collect from the pre-attack phases (Footprinting and scanning).

Metasploit

Metasploit is a Framework used for developing and executing exploit code against a remote target machine. Metasploit Framework contains following modules.

Exploits	Encoders
Payloads	Post
Auxiliary	Nop's

Components of the Metasploit:
- Msfconsole
- Msfvenom
- Armitage

Exploit

An exploit is the means by which an attacker, or pen tester for that matter, takes advantage of a flaw within a system, an application, or a service. An attacker uses an exploit to attack a system in a way that results in a particular desired outcome that the developer never intended. Common exploits include buffer overflows, web application vulnerabilities (such as SQL injection), and configuration errors.

Exploits can help gain superuser-level access to a computer system. Hackers manage to gain low-level access; then they try to escalate privileges to the highest level (root). The exploit becomes unusable; once the vulnerability is fixed through a patch.

Exploits are classified based on how the exploit communicate with the vulnerable software.

- A remote exploit works over a network and exploits the security vulnerability without any prior access to the vulnerable system.
- A local exploit requires prior access to the vulnerable system and escalate the privileges of the person running the exploit.

Payload

A payload is code that we want the system to execute and that is to be selected and delivered by the framework. For example, a reverse shell is a payload that creates a connection from the target machine back to the attacker as a windows command prompt whereas a bind shell is a payload that "binds" a command prompt to a listening port on the target machine, which the attacker can then connect. A payload could also be something as simple as a few commands to be executed on the target operating system.

Types of Payload

The Metasploit framework has three different types of payloads

1. Singles
2. Stagers
3. Stages

Single Payload
Singles are self-contained payloads. They perform a simple task like adding a user to the target computer and running executable files in the victim's computer. These kinds of payloads can be caught with non-Metasploit handlers such as netcat. These payloads are more stable because they contain everything in one.

Stager payload
Stager payloads are used to set up a network connection between the attacker and victim and provide the remote connection to execute commands. It is difficult to do both of these well, so the result is multiple similar stagers. Metasploit will use the stagers to create the buffer memory in a small portion of memory; these stagers are responsible for downloading a large payload (the stage), injecting it into memory, and passing execution to it.

Stage payload

Stage Payloads are the components of the stagers that are downloaded in the exploited pc by the Stagers. The various payload stages provide the advanced features with no size limit such as Meterpreter, VNC injection, etc.

Shellcode

Shellcode is a set of instructions used as a payload when exploitation occurs. Shellcode is typically written in assembly language. In most cases, a command shell or a Meterpreter shell will be provided after the series of instructions have been performed by the target machine, hence the name.

Module

A module in the context of this book is a piece of software that can be used by the Metasploit Framework. At times, you may require the use of an exploit, module, a software component that conducts the attack. Other times, an auxiliary module may be required to perform an action such as scanning or system enumeration. These interchangeable modules are the core of what make the Framework so powerful.

Listener

A listener is a component within Metasploit that waits for an incoming connection of some sort. For example, after the target machine has been exploited, it may call the attacking machine over the Internet. The listener handles that connection, waiting on the attacking machine to be contacted by the exploited system.

Escalating Privileges

Privilege escalation is a technique to exploit existing vulnerabilities in design, misconfigurations in an operating system or in any installed applications to gain elevated access to resources that are usually protected from an application or user.

Vertical Privilege Escalation

The attacker grants himself higher privileges. Privilege escalation is typically achieved by performing kernel-level operations that allow the attacker to run unauthorized code.

Horizontal Privilege Escalation

Attacker's use the same level of privileges he already has been granted, but assume the identity of another user with similar privileges.

Password Cracking

In password cracking, hackers use a different kind of attacks to know the target computer login password so that they can gain complete access.

Types of passwords

Passwords with only letters	:	Ex: admin
Passwords with letters and numbers	:	Ex: admin123
Passwords with letters and special characters	:	Ex: admin@
Passwords with only numbers	:	Ex: 6842
Passwords with only special characters	:	Ex: @!#$%%^
Passwords with numbers and special characters	:	Ex:1234!@#$
Passwords with letters, numbers and special characters	:	Ex: admin@123

Methods To Crack password

Password Guessing – Not a technique, but usually the first thing that every criminal will try to do.

Brute Force Attack – All possible permutations & combinations of the keyboard are tried as the victim's password. All passwords have to be some permutation or combination of victim's keyboard characters.

Dictionary Based Attack – All words in the dictionary are tried as the victim's password.

Syllable attack – Combination of both, brute force attack and a dictionary attack. This is often used when the password is a nonexistent word.

Default Passwords – Manufacturers configure the hardware or software with default passwords and settings. We can get default passwords online for devices (http://defaultpassword.us/).

Data Sniffing – Data sniffer to record passwords being sent across the LAN network in plaintext format.

Countermeasures

- Keep Operating system software updated (patched).
- Use stronger authentication methods.
- Enable security auditing to help monitor attacks.
- Avoid storing user names/password on disk.
- Change passwords on a frequent basis.
- Build user awareness on social engineering attacks.

10

Malware Threats

Malware (malicious software) is a type of program that combines malicious code with genuine application to perform unauthorized operations in such a way that it can take control of a system or cause damage.

Types of Malware

1. Trojan
2. Virus
3. Worm
4. Rootkits
5. Spyware
6. Ransomware
7. Adware
8. Backdoor

Trojan

Trojan is a malicious program, bound with a harmless application program or data in such a way that it can help an attacker gain control and cause damage to the targeted machine. Malware tries to steal victims confidential information and sends back to the attacker.

Symptoms of Trojan Attack

- Computer browser is redirected to unknown pages.
- Strange chat boxes appear on computer screen.
- Reversing the functions of the right and left mouse buttons.
- Abnormal activity by the modem, network adapter, or hard drive.
- The account passwords changes.

- The ISP complains to the target that your computer is performing unauthorized network scanning.

- An attacker can gain access to personal information about a target

Trojan Detection

- Scan for suspicious OPEN PORTS
- Scan for suspicious RUNNING PROCESSES
- Scan for suspicious DEVICE DRIVERS INSTALLED
- Scan for suspicious REGISTRY ENTRIES
- Scan for suspicious WINDOWS SERVICES
- Scan for suspicious STARTUP PROGRAMS
- Scan for suspicious NETWORK ACTIVITIES

Virus

VIRUS stands for Vital Information Resource Under Seize. The virus can self- replicate by producing a copy of itself and attaching to another program, computer boot sector or a document.

Creating a Virus using Batch file programming or bash commands
Batch file programming can be used to automate several jobs in windows operating system, which means the repetitive tasks can be written in a file by the administrators to simplify the job just by running the file instead of executing command separately.

Shell scripting performs the similar job in Linux environment to automate the execution of simple commands. Hackers take advantage of batch or shell scripting knowledge to create dangerous viruses which can destroy data on a victim machine or can consume all the PC resources to make the PC either crash or slow down.

Worms

Worms are malicious programs that replicate and spread across the network connections independently without human restrictions to infect computers

Rootkit

Rootkit is a malicious program that has the ability to hide its presence from the user (victim) and perform malicious activities to grant full access of the infected computer to the attacker.

Spyware

Spyware is a program that records user interaction with the computer, without their knowledge and sends them to the remote attackers over the internet. Spyware hides its process, files, and other objects to avoid detection and removal.

Ransomware

Ransomware is a malware that can restrict access to computer system files and folders and demands an online ransom payment to the malware creator to remove the restrictions.

Adware

Adware is designed to display unwanted advertisements on the browser which redirects users search requests to malicious web pages that forces them to download malware on to their computers. Adware can also be used to collect users search habits.

Backdoor

A backdoor is a piece of code executed on victim computer system by an attacker to bypass standard authentication and maintain secure unauthorized access to remote desktop.

Countermeasures

- Do not download email attachments received from unknown senders.
- Block unnecessary ports running vulnerable services.
- Avoid downloading and executing applications from untrusted sources.
- Restrict permissions within the desktop environment to prevent malicious applications installation.
- Run host-based antivirus, firewall, and intrusion detection software.
- Manage local workstation file integrity through checksums, auditing, and port scanning.

11

Sniffing

Sniffing is the process of monitoring and capturing all data packets passing through a given network. Sniffing is a form of wiretap applied to computer networks. We can sniff data packets using tools like Wireshark. Any protocol that do not encrypt data are vulnerable to sniffing attacks. Attackers use sniffers to capture data packets containing sensitive information such as passwords, account information, etc.

Sniffers Works in the Datalink Layer. If the initial layer is compromised, then the rest of the layers are also compromised in the OSI model

Sniffer

A sniffer is a software tool that monitors the data flowing through computer network links in real time. It can be a self-contained software program or a hardware device with the appropriate software or firmware to perform sniffing.

Sniffers can capture copies of data packets without redirecting or altering it. Some sniffers work only with TCP/IP packets, but the more sophisticated tools can work with many other network protocols and at lower levels, including ethernet frames.

Types of sniffing

Sniffing is classified into two types based on the way they interact with the data packet to capture and provide the user the ability to alter the packet.

- Active sniffing
- Passive sniffing

Active Sniffing

Active Sniffing involves injecting address resolution (ARP) packets into the network to modify Content Addressable Memory (CAM) Table which resides in the switch; CAM keeps track of which host is connected to which port on the switched network.

Passive sniffing

Passive sniffing involves listening and capturing traffic, in a network connected by hubs.

Protocols Vulnerable to Sniffing

HTTP – 80	FTP – 20/21
POP3 – 110	SMTP – 25
RDP – 3389	SSH – 22
NTP – 123	Telnet – 23
IMAP – 123	SNMP - 25

Port Mirroring (SPAN port)

Port mirroring is used by the network switch to send a copy of all network traffic to SPAN port on the switch. This is commonly used for monitoring network traffic by system administrators to detect suspicious activities in the network.

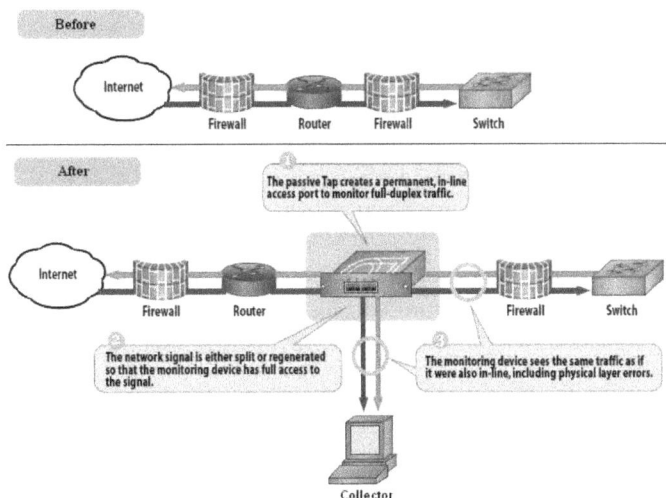

Address Resolution Protocol

Address Resolution Protocol (ARP) is a communication protocol used for discovering the link layer address, such as a MAC address, associated with a given network layer address. This mapping is a critical function in the Internet Protocol suite. It is communicated within the boundaries of a single network never routed across internetworking nodes. ARP uses a simple message format containing one address resolution request or response. The size of the ARP message depends on the link layer and network layer address sizes.

ARP spoofing

In computer networking, ARP spoofing is a technique by which an attacker sends spoofed ARP messages onto a local area network. Generally, the aim is to associate the attacker's MAC address with the IP address of another host, such as the default gateway, causing any traffic meant for that IP address to be sent to the attacker instead. ARP spoofing may allow an attacker to intercept data frames on a network, modify the traffic, or stop all traffic. Often this attack leads to other attacks, such as

Denial of service (DoS), Man in the middle (MITM), or Session hijacking attacks.

DNS spoofing

DNS spoofing is a technique of introducing corrupt Domain Name System details into the DNS resolver cache causing the name server to return an incorrect result record. This results in traffic being diverted to the attacker's computer.

A domain name system translates human-readable domain name into a numerical IP address that is used to route communications between nodes. If a DNS server is poisoned, it returns an incorrect IP address that diverts the traffic to another computer.

Man in the Middle attack

Man in the Middle attack is where an attacker positions himself in a conversation between a user and an application either to eavesdrop or to impersonate regular conversations. The attacker tries to steal personal information, such as login credentials, account details, and credit card numbers. Information obtained during attacks can be used to perform identity theft, unapproved fund transfers or an illicit password change.

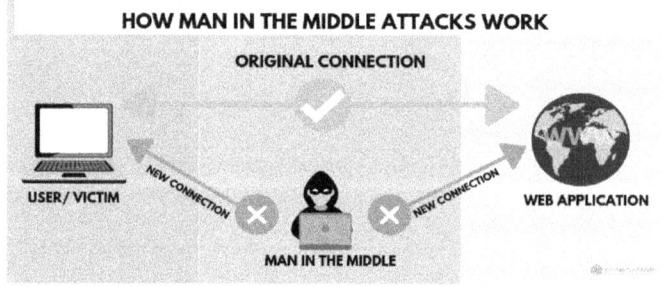

Sniffing Detection Methods

1. Observing Network Traffic
2. Observing ARP Table to Detect ARP Poisoning
3. XARP Advanced ARP Poisoning Detection Tool

Countermeasures

- Use HTTPS instead of HTTP to protect usernames and passwords.

- Use switch instead of the hub as switch delivers data only to the intended recipient.

- Use SFTP, instead of FTP for secure transfer of files.

- Use PGP and S/MIME, VPN, IPSec, SSL/TLS, SSH and One-time passwords.

- Always encrypt the wireless traffic with a strong encryption protocol such as WPA and WPA2.

- Retrieve MAC directly from NIC instead of OS; this prevents MAC address spoofing.

- Use tools to determine if any NIC's are running in the promiscuous mode.

12

Social Engineering

Social engineering

Social engineering is an art of exploiting humans to gain sensitive information. This technique involves tricking people into breaking standard security procedures. It is a most significant threat in any organization. Common targets of social engineering include help desk personnel, technical support executives, system administrators, etc.

Types of Social engineering

Social engineering is classified based on the techniques used to attack or commit fraud on the victim to steal the sensitive information. Types of social engineering attacks are:

- Human-based
- Computer-based
- Mobile-based

Human-Based

In human-based social engineering attacks, the social engineer interacts directly with the target to get sensitive information by performing the various techniques such as

- Shoulder surfing
- Dumpster diving
- Tailgating
- Piggybacking

Computer Based

Computer-based social engineering attacks are carried out with the help of computer software to gain access to the desired information. Some of these attack types are listed as follows:

- Phishing
- Spam mail
- Popup windows

Mobile Based

In mobile-based social engineering attacks, attackers take advantage of malicious mobile applications to gain access to the desired information. Some of the attack types are listed as follows:

- SMishing
- Publish malicious apps
- Repacking legitimate apps

Exploiting Human Using Social engineering

Social engineering and the human element are common ways to gain access to a network, database, or building. Major cyber incidents happen as the result of an attacker gaining initial access using social engineering technique, usually by convincing an insider to unwittingly download or install a piece of malware that opens up the target network to the attacker.

Attackers employ many tricks to try to get a human target to provide them with information or access. They appeal to ego, financial need, curiosity, humanity, or job duties all with the goal of getting the target to either click on a link that redirects the target to a malicious website or opens an attachment that contains malware.

Humans continue to be the weak link. No matter how secure a network, device, system, or organization is from a technical point of view, humans can often be exploited.

- Individuals should be vigilant regarding emails
- unsolicited phone calls that attempt to get people to reveal sensitive information.
- Companies should regularly provide security awareness training to employees.
- Lack of the security policies
- Unregulated access to information

Eavesdropping

Eavesdropping is a technique used by attackers to intercept unauthorized and private communication, such as a phone call, instant message, video conference or fax transmission. This is done by directly listening to digital or analog voice communication or by intercepting or sniffing data relating to any form of communication.

Dumpster diving

Dumpster diving is looking for treasure in someone else's trash. (A dumpster is a large trash container). In Information Technology, dumpster diving refers to a technique used to retrieve information that could be used to perform attacks on a computer network. Dumpster diving is not limited to searching through the trash for information like access codes or passwords written down on sticky notes

Shoulder Surfing

Shoulder surfing is noting but direct observation, such as looking over someone's shoulder, to grab sensitive details. It is commonly used while someone enters passwords, PIN numbers, security codes at ATMs or on their personal computers.

Tailgating and Piggybacking

A person tags himself with another person who is authorized to gain access into a restricted area, or pass a specific checkpoint is known as Tailgating/Piggybacking. Tailgating implies without consent while piggybacking means approval of the authorized person.

Phishing

Phishing is the attempt to acquire sensitive information such as usernames, passwords, and credit card details (and sometimes, financial information), often for malicious reasons, by masquerading as a trustworthy entity in electronic communication.

Spear phishing

Spear phishing is a variation on phishing in which hackers send emails to groups of people with specific common characteristics or other identifiers. Spear phishing emails appear to come from a trusted source but are designed to help hackers obtain trade secrets or other classified information.

Countermeasures

1. Employees in an organization should be aware of security policies and procedures.
2. Secure or shred all the documents containing private information.
3. Protect your personal information from being published.
4. Never store personal/banking information on the mobile device.

13

DoS And DDoS Attack

Denial of Service

Denial of Service (DoS) attack is an attempt to make a machine or network resource unavailable to its intended users, such as to temporarily or indefinitely interrupt or suspend services of a host connected to the Internet.

Distributed Denial Of service

Distributed Denial-of-Service (DDoS) attack occurs when multiple systems flood the targeted system with traffic to make the resources unavailable to its intended users, usually one or more web servers. Such an attack is often the result of multiple compromised systems for example a botnet flooding attack.

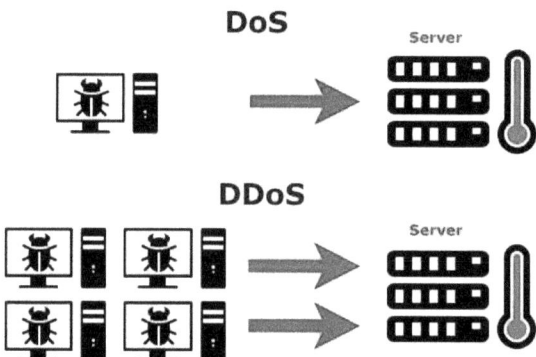

Botnet

A botnet is a collection of Internet-connected devices that are infected and controlled by a common type of malware each of which is running one or more bots. Infected machines are controlled remotely. Botnet infections are usually spread through malware, such as a trojan horse. Botnet malware is typically designed to automatically scan systems and devices for common vulnerabilities that haven't been patched. Botnet malware may also scan for ineffective or outdated security products, such as firewalls or antivirus software. Common tasks executed by botnets include

- Using the machine's power to assist in distributed denial-of-service (DDoS).
- Generating spam emails.
- Internet traffic generation on a third-party website.

Replacing banner ads in a web browser

Exploiting System and Application Level Vulnerabilities

In this method, either the operating system or the application software will have bugs which will cause a denial of service situation. Once an attacker finds this vulnerability, he has to find out the working exploit code for the vulnerability, if an attacker finds the exploit code he can use it to DOS the target without any further problems.

TCP SYN Flood

TCP SYN flood is a type of Distributed Denial of Service (DDoS) attack that exploits part of the normal TCP three-way handshake to consume resources on the targeted server and render it unresponsive. With SYN flood DDoS, the attacker sends TCP connection requests faster than the targeted machine can process them, causing network saturation.

In a SYN flood attack, the attacker sends repeated SYN packets to every port on the targeted server, using a fake IP address. The server receives multiple, apparently legitimate requests to establish communication. It responds to each attempt with a SYN-ACK packet from each open port.

The attacker either does not send the expected ACK or if the IP address is spoofed never receives the SYN-ACK in the first place. Either way, the server under attack will wait for an acknowledgment for its SYN-ACK packet for some time. During this time, the server cannot close down the connection by sending RST packet, and the connection stays open. Before the connection can time out, another SYN packet will arrive. This leaves an increasingly large number of connections half-open

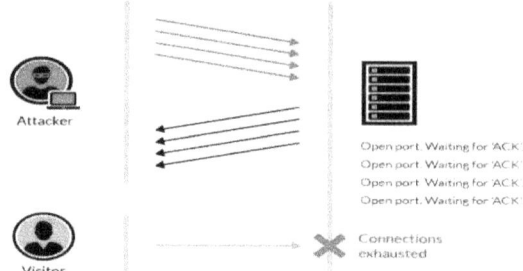

UDP Flood

UDP flood is a type of Denial of Service (DoS) attack in which the attacker sends a request to random ports on the targeted host with IP packets containing UDP datagrams.

The receiving host checks for applications associated with these datagrams and if no application is associated with the request, then it sends back a "Destination Unreachable" packet. As more and more UDP packets are received which need to be answered, the system becomes overwhelmed and unresponsive to other clients. The attacker may also spoof the IP address of the packets, both to make sure that the return ICMP packets do not reach their host, to anonymize the attack.

User Datagram Protocol (UDP) is a connectionless and session less networking protocol. Since UDP traffic does not require a three-way handshake like TCP, it runs with lower overhead and is ideal for traffic that does not need to be checked and rechecked, such as chat or VoIP.

In the absence of an initial handshake, to establish a valid connection, a high volume of traffic can be sent over UDP channels to any host, with no built-in protection to limit the rate of the UDP DoS flood. This means that UDP flood attacks are highly-effective.

Some UDP flood attacks can take the form of DNS amplification attacks. Where UDP does not define specific packet formats, and thus attackers can create large packets fill them with junk text or numbers and send them out to the host under attack.

When the attacked host receives the garbage-filled UDP packets to a given port, it checks for the application listening at that port, which is associated with the packet's contents. When it observes that, no associated application is listening, it replies with an ICMP Destination Unreachable packet

HTTP Flood

HTTP flood is a type of Distributed Denial of Service (DDoS) attack in which the attacker sends seemingly legitimate HTTP GET or POST requests to a target web server or application. HTTP client like a web browser communicates with application or server; it sends an HTTP request. A GET request is used to retrieve content while POST requests are used to send dynamically generated content.

The attack is effective when it forces the server or application to allocate the maximum resources possible in response to every single request. For this reason, HTTP flood attacks using POST requests tend to be the most resource effective. POST requests may include parameters that trigger complex server-side processing. On the other hand, HTTP GET based attacks are simple to perform.

Ping of Death

In this method of DOS, the attacker will try to send the large-sized ping packets which the target cannot handle which will cause DOS situation on the target device.

MAC Flooding

The Network switch maintains a table called CAM (content addressable memory) to prevent MITM attacks, but it contains a limited number of entries, so when an attacker tries to overload this CAM table with more number of mac addresses than it can handle, sometimes the switch may not be responding to the legitimate requests.

Other types of Flooding

An attacker can use any other protocol vulnerabilities to flood packets to the target device so that the target device will be busy with handling Flood packets and may not respond to the original request made by the legitimate user.

Countermeasures

- DoS detection techniques are based on identifying and discriminating the illegitimate traffic from legitimate packet traffic

- Set up Systems with limited security (Honeypots), to attract an attacker

- FortGuard Anti-DDoS Firewall provides a fundamentally superior approach to mitigating DDoS attacks, with a design that focuses on passing legitimate traffic rather than discarding attack traffic.

14

Session Hijacking

A session stores information (in variables) to be used across multiple pages when a user logs into this online account. Unlike cookies, this information is not stored on the user's computer. Typically maintained by the server, and created on the first request or after an authentication process. The session-id is exchanged between a web browser and the server on every request.

Different ways to exchange session-Id
1. Hidden form fields
2. Cookies (most common)

Session Token

Session ID or session token is a piece of data that is used in network communications to identify a session. It is used to determine a user that has logged into a website, these IDS or token can be used by an attacker to hijack the session and obtain potential privileges. A session ID is usually a randomly generated string to decrease the probability of obtaining a valid one by means of a brute-force search.

Cookie

Cookies are strings of data that a web server sends to the browser. When a browser requests an object from the same domain in the future, the browser will send the same string of date back to the origin server. The data sent from the web server in the form of an HTTP header called "Set-Cookie". The browser sends the cookie back to the server in an HTTP header called "Cookie".

The primary purpose of a cookie is to create customized web pages based on user identities.

Attack Methods

- Guessing Session Id - shorter length, predictable
- Session Fixing - predictable, session created before authentication
- Session Sniffing (typical on non-SSL sessions) - same subnet as client or server.
- Cross Site Scripting (XSS) - User trusting source, application vulnerability.

Session Sniffing

Attackers can sniff all the traffic from the established TCP session and perform identity theft, information theft, fraud, etc. The attacker steals a valid session ID and uses it to authenticate himself with the server.

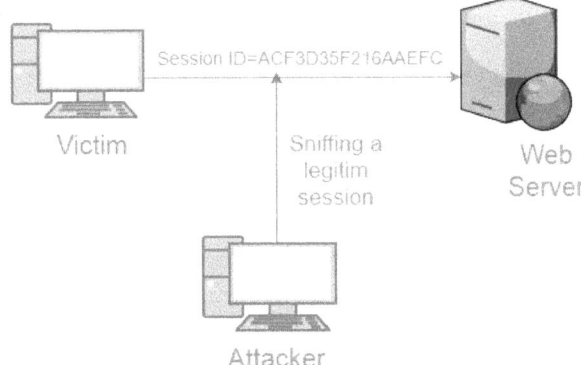

Session Hijacking

Session Hijacking refers stealing of this session-Id and using it to impersonate and access data over a valid TCP communication session between two computers. Application level hijacking is about gaining control over the HTTP user session by obtaining the session IDs.

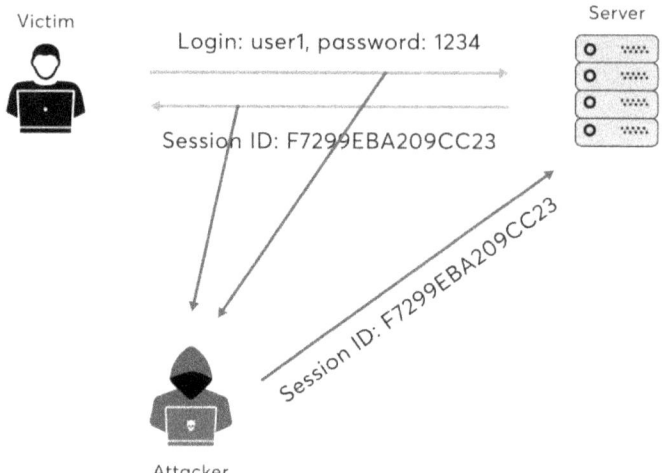

Countermeasures from a general user point of view

- Do not click on the links that are received through emails.
- Logout from the application instead of closing the browser.
- Always use an updated b rowser.
- Clear the browsing data like cache, cookies, etc.

Countermeasures from web developer point of view

- Create Session keys with lengthy strings or random number so that it is difficult for an attacker to guess a valid session key.
- Regenerate the session ID after a successful login to prevent session fixation attack (attack starts before user logs in).
- Encrypt the data and session key that is transferred between the user and the web servers.
- Expire the session as soon as the user logs out.
- Use firewalls to prevent the malicious content entering into the network.

15

Firewalls, Honeypots, IDS & IPS

Firewall is a hardware or software appliance to secure the internal trusted network form the intruders by monitoring and controlling incoming and outgoing network traffic based on predetermined security rules. A firewall typically establishes a barrier between a trusted internal network and an untrusted external network.

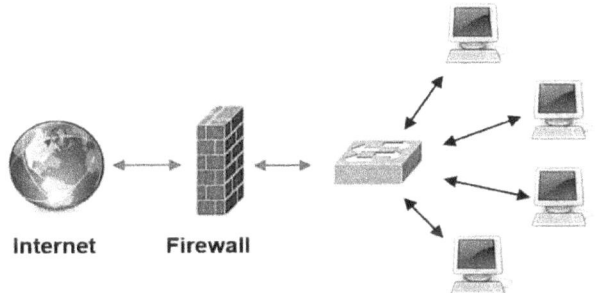

Types of Firewalls

1. Packet filter firewalls
2. Circuit-level gateways
3. Stateful inspection firewalls
4. Application-level gateways

Packet Filter Firewalls

Packet filtering firewall is used to control network access by monitoring outgoing and incoming packets and allowing them to pass or halt based on the source and destination Internet Protocol (IP) addresses, protocols and ports and this work on IP layer of TCP/IP. The packet filtering firewall examines the header of each packet based on a specific set of rules.

Circuit-level gateways

Circuit level gateways work at the session layer of the OSI model; they monitor TCP handshake to determine whether a requested session is legitimate or not. Information passed to a remote computer through a circuit level gateway firewall appears to be originated at user's computer. Firewall technology supervises TCP handshaking among packets to confirm that the session is genuine.

Circuit level gateways are relatively inexpensive and have the advantage of hiding information about the private network. On the other hand, they do not filter individual packets.

Application-level gateways

Application-level gateways can filter packets at the application layer of the OSI model. Application-level gateways examine traffic and filter on application specific commands such as HTTP, POST and GET. This works on the application layer of the TCP/IP Model.

Stateful inspection firewalls

Stateful inspection firewalls combine the aspects of the other three types of firewalls. They filter packets at the network layer, to determine whether session packets are legitimate, and they evaluate the contents of packets at the application layer. Traffic is filtered at three layers based on a wide range of the specified application, session, and packet filtering rules.

Types of Firewall Architectures

The different types of firewall architectures are

1. Bastion Host
2. Screened Subnet (DMZ - Demilitarized Zone)
3. Dual-Homed Firewall

Bastion Host

A Bastion host is a computer that is fully exposed to attack. The system is on the public side of the demilitarized zone, unprotected by a firewall or filtering router. Frequently the roles of these systems are critical to the network security system.

The Complete Ethical Hacking Book

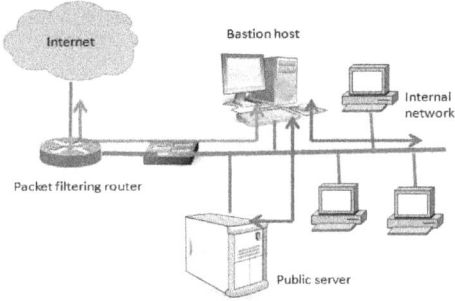

Screened host firewall (single-homed bastion host)

Screened Subnet (DMZ)

A screened subnet (also known as a "triple-homed firewall") is a network architecture that uses a single firewall with three network interfaces. In computer security, a DMZ or demilitarized zone is a physical or logical subnetwork that contains and exposes an organization's external-facing services to a larger and untrusted network, usually the Internet.

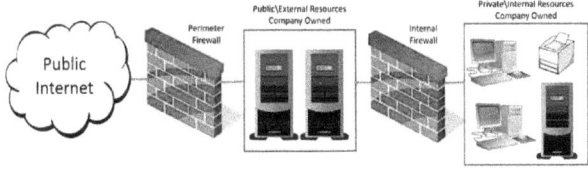

Dual-Homed Firewall

A dual-homed host (or dual-homed gateway) is a system fitted with two network interfaces (NICs) that sits between an untrusted network (like the Internet) and trusted network (such as a corporate network) to provide secure access. Dual- homed is a general term for proxies, gateways, firewalls, or any server running security applications or providing security services directly to an untrusted network.

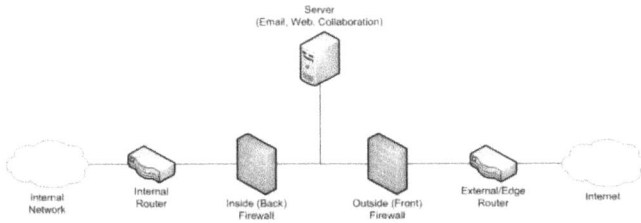

Dual-homed hosts can be seen as a special case of bastion hosts and multi-homed hosts. They fall into the category of application-based firewalls. Dual-homed hosts can act as firewalls provided that they do not forward IP datagrams unconditionally.

List of Firewall Products

Software Firewalls	Hardware Firewalls
Windows Firewall	FortiGate NGFW
ZoneAlarm	Check Point NGFW
Nftables	Sophos XG
IPFilter	WatchGuard Network Security
Norton 360	SonicWall
PeerBlock	Cisco
Shorewall	GlassWire Firewall
NetLimiter	Avast
Lavasoft personal firewall	Zscaler Internet Access
Netfilter etc..	Juniper etc..

Honeypot

In computer terminology, a honeypot is a computer security mechanism set to detect or deflect attempts at unauthorized access to the information systems. In other words, it is a simple trap to catch the hackers. In honeypots, we will emulate the required devices in an environment, and we will let attackers come there and try to perform attacks. But meanwhile, we will get the identity of the attacker. So that we can take action against attacks. Honeypots are of two types.

Low Interaction Honeypot

Low interaction honeypots allow only limited interaction for an attacker. All services offered by a low interaction honeypot are emulated. Thus, these are not themselves vulnerable and will not become infected by the exploit attempted against the vulnerability.

High interaction honeypot

High interaction honeypots make use of the actual vulnerable service or software. These are usually complex as they involve real vulnerable operating systems and applications. In this type of Honeypots, nothing is emulated everything is real and provide a far more detailed picture of how an attack or intrusion progresses or how a particular malware executes in real-time.

List of honeypots

Database Honeypots

- Elastic honey - A simple elastic search honeypot
- NoSQL Honeypot Framework - A framework for NoSQL databases
- ESPot - elasticsearch honeypot

Anti-honeypot stuff

- Kippo detect - This is not a honeypot, but it detects kippo.

ICS/SCADA honeypots

- Conpot - ICS/SCADA honeypot
- Scada-honeynet - Mimics many of the services from a popular PLC and better helps SCADA researchers understand the potential risks of exposed control system devices

Service Honeypots

- Honey NTP - NTP logger/honeypot
- Honeypot camera - Observation camera honeypot
- Troje - A honeypot built around lxc containers. It will run each connection with the service within a separate lxc container.
- Slipm honeypot - A simple low-interaction port monitoring honeypot

Web honeypots

- Glastopf - Web Application Honeypot
- PhpMyAdmin honeypot - A simple and effective phpMyAdmin honeypot
- Servlet pot - Web Application Honeypot

- Node pot - A Nodejs web app NoSQL honeypot framework application

- Basic Auth Pot - HTTP basic authentication honeypot

- Shadow Daemon - A modular Web Application Firewall / High-Interaction Honeypot for PHP, Perl & Python apps

- Google Hack Honeypot - designed to provide reconnaissance against attackers that use search engines as a hacking tool against your resources.

- Smart Honeypot - PHP script demonstrating a smart honeypot

- WP Smart Honeypot - WordPress plugin to reduce comment spam with a smarter honeypot

- Word pot - A WordPress Honeypot

- Bukkit Honeypot - A honeypot plugin for Bukkit

- Laravel Application Honeypot - Simple spam prevention package for Laravel applications

- Stack Honeypot - Inserts a trap for spambots into responses

- Eos Honeypot Bundle - Honeypot type for Symfony2 forms

- Shock pot - WebApp Honeypot for detecting Shell Shock exploit attempts

Intrusion Detection System (IDS)

An intrusion detection system (IDS) is a device or software application that monitors network or computer system operations for malicious activities, policy violations and reports to a controlling station.

Capabilities of IDS
- Monitoring the operation of routers, firewalls, key management servers and files that are needed by other security controls aimed at detecting, preventing or recovering from cyber attacks.

- Including an extensive attack signature database against which information from the system can be matched.

- Recognizing and reporting when the IDS detects that data files have been altered.

- Generating an alarm and notifying the security operations team when there is a security breach.

IDS detection methods

Signature-based

Signature-based IDS performs detection of attacks by looking for specific patterns, such as byte sequences in network traffic, or known malicious instruction sequences used by malware. Signature-based IDS is very helpful for detecting already known attacks, but it fails in detecting new attacks, for which no pattern is available. Signatures fall into two categories

Attack signatures - They describe action patterns that may pose a security threat. Typically, they are presented as a time-dependent relationship between a series of activities.

Selected text strings - Signatures to match text strings which look for suspicious action (for example - calling /etc./passwd)

Anomaly-based

Anomaly detectors construct profiles that represent normal usage and then use current behavior data to detect a possible mismatch between profiles and recognize possible attack attempts. In order to match event profiles, the system is required to produce initial user profiles to train the system about legitimate user behaviors, which is a difficult and time-consuming task. Everything that does not match the stored profile is considered to be a suspicious action.

Types of IDS

1. Network-based Intrusion Detection System
2. Host-based Intrusion Detection System

Network-based IDS

NIDS is an IDS which can be configured on a network to monitor intrusions. This will notify the administrators about any possible signature match of attacks.

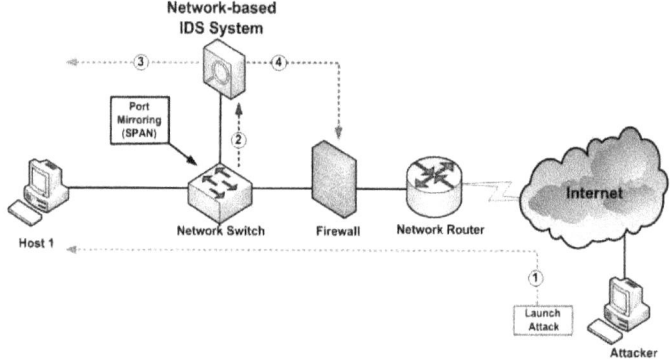

Host-based IDS

HIDS are the IDS systems which will be configured on the standalone machines and will only detect intrusions for that particular machine.

HIDS might detect which program accesses what resources and discover malicious attempts, for example, a word-processor has suddenly started modifying the system password database, which can be considered as a malicious attempt on sensitive data stored on the host machine.

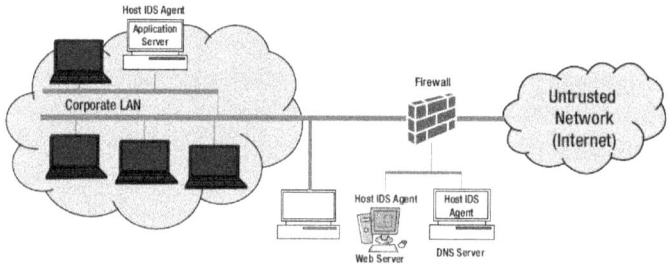

List of Intrusion detection systems

- Snort IDS
- SonicWall
- Juniper
- McAfee Security Agent
- Palo Alto
- Cisco ASA Security Agent ..etc

Intrusion Prevention System (IPS)

An Intrusion Prevention System (IPS) is a network security/threat prevention technology that examines network traffic flows to detect and prevent vulnerability exploits. Vulnerability exploits usually come in the form of malicious inputs to a target application or service that attackers use to interrupt and gain control of an application or machine.

The IPS often sits directly behind the firewall and provides a complementary layer of analysis for dangerous content detection. The Intrusion Detection System (IDS) which is a passive system that scans traffic and reports back on threats but the Intrusion Prevention System (IPS) is placed in the direct communication path between source and destination, that can actively analyze and take automated actions on all traffic that enter the network. These actions include:

- Sending an alarm to the administrator
- Dropping the malicious packets
- Blocking traffic from the source address
- Resetting the connection

Types of IPS

Host-based intrusion prevention systems

Host-based intrusion prevention systems are used to protect both servers and workstations through software that runs between your system's applications and OS kernel. The software is preconfigured to determine the protection rules based on intrusion and attack signatures. The HIPS will catch suspicious activity on the system and then, depend on the predefined rules; it will either block or allow the event to happen. HIPS monitor activities such as application or data requests, network connection attempts, and read or write attempts.

Network-based intrusion prevention systems

Network-based intrusion prevention system is a solution for network-based security. NIPS will intercept all network traffic and monitor it for suspicious activity and events, either blocking the requests or passing it. One interesting aspect of NIPS is that if the system finds an offending packet of information it can rewrite the packet so that attempt for the attack will fail, but the organization can mark this event to gather evidence against the intruder, without their knowledge.

Countermeasures

- Shut down switch ports associated with the known attack hosts.
- Perform an in-depth analysis of network traffic to detect all possible threats.
- Use a traffic normalizer to remove potential ambiguity from the packet stream before it reaches to the IDS.
- Harden the security of all communication devices such as modems, routers, switches, etc.

16

Hacking Web Servers

Web Server

Web Server is a computing system that runs on server OS to process the HTTP/HTTPS requests and serve the web pages on the world wide web. The pages delivered are HTML documents, which may include images and scripts in addition to the text content. Clients use a web browser to interact with the web server.

Any computer can be turned into a Web server by installing server software and connecting the machine to the Internet. There are many Web server software applications like Xampp, Apache, Nginx, IIS web server, etc.

How Web Servers Work?

When a user requests a web page hosted on the internet, the web server responds with that requested page. The below image represents this process.

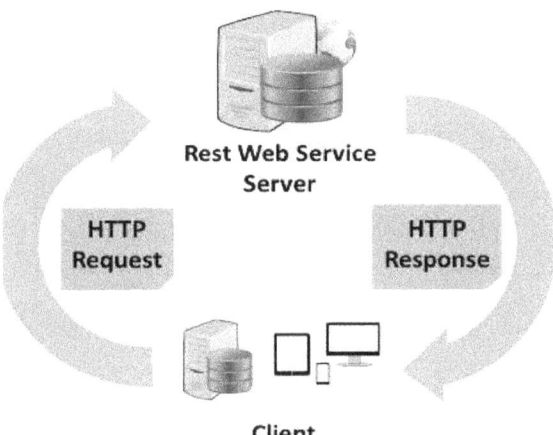

Obtaining the IP Address from domain name: Web browser first obtains the domain name and resolves it to IP address. It can obtain the IP address in 2 ways:

1. By searching cache.
2. By requesting one or more DNS Servers.

After knowing the IP Address, the browser now demands a full URL from the web server. The web server responds, by sending the requested page to the browser, and if, the web page does not exist, then it will display an appropriate error message. The browser renders the response received from the server to display it on the screen.

List of popular web servers

The following are a list of the common web servers:

Apache – The commonly used web server on the internet. It is cross-platform application software, but it is usually installed on Linux. Most PHP websites are hosted on Apache servers.

Internet Information Services (IIS) – It runs on windows and is the second most used web server on the internet. Most websites built using ASP.Net are hosted on IIS servers.

Apache Tomcat – Java server pages (JSP) websites are hosted on this type of web server.

Other web servers – Novell's Web Server, IBM Lotus Domino servers, Cloudflare web server, Oracle web server, Lightspeed servers, Amazon web server, Google web server, Nginx, etc.

Footprinting Web Server

- Attackers use ID Serve, Netcraft, HTTP Recon, Whois tools to get details about the target server.
- Use robot's exclusion protocol, a standard used by websites to communicate with web crawlers and other web robots to gather some sensitive information.
- This file (robots.txt) will inform the web robot about which areas of the website should not be processed or scanned.
- By performing the DNS enumeration, we can get the dns records and types of servers.

Web Server Vulnerabilities

The following vulnerabilities are most commonly exploited in web servers:

- Improper file and directory permissions.

- Unnecessary services enabled, including content management and remote administration.

- Improper authentication with external systems.

- Default accounts with default or no passwords.

- Misconfiguration in web-server, operating system or network.

- Bugs in server software, OS or web application.

- Lack of security policy and procedures

Types of Attacks possible against Web Servers

Denial of Service Attacks – With this type of attack, the web server may crash or become unavailable to the legitimate users.

Domain Name System Hijacking – In this type of attack, the DNS settings are changed to point victims to the attacker's web server. All the traffic was supposed to hit a malicious server.

Sniffing – Unencrypted data sent over the network may be intercepted and used to gain unauthorized access to the web server.

Defacement – In this type of attack, the attacker takes advantage of vulnerabilities in the web server to replaces the organization's website with a different page that contains the hacker's name, images and may include background music and messages.

Impact of Web Server Attacks

- Easy to compromise user accounts.

- Gaining root access to other applications on servers.

- Access to confidential data (Data tampering/Data theft).

- Perform Web Application attacks.

- The compromised web server can be used to spread malicious software on the internet, which can infect users who visit the compromised website.

- Compromised user data can be used for fraudulent activities.

- An organization's reputation can be ruined.

Identify Vulnerabilities on Web Server

- Perform vulnerability scan to identify weaknesses in a network and determine if the system can be exploited.

- Use vulnerability scanners like Sparta, Nikto, HP Web Inspect, Acunetix Web Vulnerability Scanner to find out hosts, services, and vulnerabilities.

- Sniff the network traffic to identify vulnerabilities on active systems or network services.

- Test the web server infrastructure for any misconfigurations, outdated content, and vulnerabilities.

Countermeasures

- Scan for existing vulnerabilities, patch and update the server software regularly.

- Block all unnecessary ports, ICMP traffic, and unnecessary protocols.

- Consistently apply the latest software patches and update system software.

- If remote access is needed, make sure that the remote connection is adequately secured, by using tunneling and encryption protocols.

- Stop running vulnerable applications on the server, such as WebDAV. Unnecessary applications can be removed on a server by using Add/Remove Programs in the Windows Control Panel.

- Perform bound checking on input for web forms and query strings to prevent buffer overflow or malicious input attacks.

- Disable remote administration.

- Avoid printing error messages.

- Enable auditing and logging.

- Use a firewall between the web server and the Internet and allow only necessary ports (such as 80 and 443) through the firewall.

- Replace the GET method with the POST method when sending data to a web server.

17

Hacking Web Applications

Web Application

A Web Application is a program that is accessed over a network connection using HTTP or HTTPS existing in the web server. The web application is a client- server application which client run in web browser. The web application contains a set of web pages, scripts, images, etc. Web applications help organizations to grow their business.

Types of websites

Static Website:
A static website contains web pages with fixed content. A static site can be built using HTML and hosted on a Web server.

Dynamic Website:
The information on dynamic website changes based on user interaction, the time zone, the viewer's native language, and other factors. These pages include Web scripting code, such as PHP or ASP. When a dynamic page is accessed, the code within the page is parsed on the Web server, and the resulting HTML is sent to the client web browser. Dynamic websites can interact with the user, capable of access information stored on the database. Dynamic web pages are also known as database-driven websites.

How A Web Application Works

- The user sends a request to the web server over the internet through the web browser or the application interface in the form of URL or an HTML form

- Web server forward these requests to the web application server

- Web application server queries the database and generates the results for the requested task

- Web servers respond back to the client with the requested information

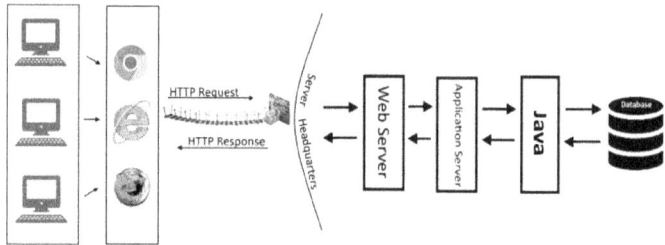

OWASP

The Open Web Application Security Project (OWASP), an online community, produces freely-available articles, methodologies, documentation, tools, and technologies in the field of web application security. It aims to raise awareness about application security by identifying some of the most critical risks that organizations are facing.

OWASP Top 10 Web Application Security Risks (2021)

A01:2021	Broken Access Control
A02:2021	Cryptographic Failures
A03: 2021	Injection
A04:2021	Insecure Design
A05:2021	Security Misconfiguration
A06:2021	Vulnerable and outdated Components
A07:2021	Identification and Authentication Failures
A08:2021	Software and Data Integrity Failures
A09:2021	Security Logging and Monitoring Failures
A10:2021	Server-Side Request Forgery

A01:2021-Broken Access Control moves up from the fifth position; 94% of applications were tested for some form of broken access control. The 34 Common Weakness Enumerations (CWEs) mapped to Broken Access Control had more occurrences in applications than any other category.

A02:2021-Cryptographic Failures shifts up one position to #2, previously known as Sensitive Data Exposure, which was broad symptom rather than a root cause. The renewed focus here is on failures related to cryptography which often leads to sensitive data exposure or system compromise.

A03:2021-Injection slides down to the third position. 94% of the applications were tested for some form of injection, and the 33 CWEs mapped into this category have the second most occurrences in applications. Cross-site Scripting is now part of this category in this edition.

A04:2021-Insecure Design is a new category for 2021, with a focus on risks related to design flaws. If we genuinely want to "move left" as an industry, it calls for more use of threat modeling, secure design patterns and principles, and reference architectures.

A05:2021-Security Misconfiguration moves up from #6 in the previous edition; 90% of applications were tested for some form of misconfiguration. With more shifts into highly configurable software, it's not surprising to see this category move up. The former category for XML External Entities (XXE) is now part of this category.

A06:2021-Vulnerable and Outdated Components was previously titled Using Components with Known Vulnerabilities and is #2 in the Top 10 community survey, but also had enough data to make the Top 10 via data analysis. This category moves up from #9 in 2017 and is a known issue that we struggle to test and assess risk. It is the only category not to have any Common Vulnerability and Exposures (CVEs) mapped to the included CWEs, so a default exploit and impact weights of 5.0 are factored into their scores.

A07:2021-Identification and Authentication Failures was previously Broken Authentication and is sliding down from the second position, and now includes CWEs that are more related to identification failures. This category is still an integral part of the Top 10, but the increased availability of standardized frameworks seems to be helping.

A08:2021-Software and Data Integrity Failures is a new category for 2021, focusing on making assumptions related to software updates, critical data, and CI/CD pipelines without verifying integrity. One of the highest weighted impacts from Common Vulnerability and Exposures/Common Vulnerability Scoring System (CVE/CVSS) data mapped to the 10 CWEs in this category. Insecure Deserialization from 2017 is now a part of this larger category.

A09:2021-Security Logging and Monitoring Failures was previously Insufficient Logging & Monitoring and is added from the industry survey (#3), moving up from #10 previously. This category is expanded to include more types of failures, is challenging to test for, and isn't well represented in the CVE/CVSS data. However, failures in this category can directly impact visibility, incident alerting, and forensics.

A10:2021-Server-Side Request Forgery is added from the Top 10 community survey (#1). The data shows a relatively low incidence rate with above average testing coverage, along with above-average ratings for Exploit and Impact potential. This category represents the scenario where the security community members are telling us this is important, even though it's not illustrated in the data at this time.

Cross-site scripting attack

- XSS attack takes advantage of dynamically generated web content based on user input provided on web pages.
- An attacker tries to inject commands in input fields provided on web pages.
- If the web server is unable to validate input fields on a web page properly, then it will execute the command provided by the attacker and unknowingly reveal information related to the client.

Types of XSS
1. Cross-site scripting (Reflected)
2. Cross-site scripting (Stored)
3. Cross-site scripting (DOM)

1. **Insecure Deserialization:** Insecure deserialization often leads to remote code execution. Even if deserialization flaws do not result in remote code execution, they can be used to perform attacks, including replay attacks, injection attacks, and privilege escalation attacks.

2. **Using Components with Known Vulnerabilities:** Components, such as libraries, frameworks, and other software modules, run with the same privileges as the application. If a vulnerable component is exploited, such an attack can facilitate serious data loss or server takeover. Applications and APIs using components with known vulnerabilities may undermine application defenses and enable various attacks and impacts.

3. **Insufficient Logging & Monitoring:** Insufficient logging and monitoring, coupled with missing or ineffective integration with incident response, allows attackers to further attack systems, maintain persistence, pivot to more systems, and tamper,

extract, or destroy data. Most breach studies show time to detect a breach is over 200 days, typically detected by external parties rather than internal processes or monitoring.

Parameter Tampering

This attack involves the manipulation of parameters exchanged between client and server to modify application data such as user credentials, permissions, price, the quantity of products. Establishing a proxy can make the process of tampering simple if the web application fails in proper session management.

Directory Traversal

- Directory Traversal or Path Traversal is an attack on HTTP which allows attackers to access restricted directories outside of the web server root location.

- Attackers try to access restricted directories that contain sensitive information like server configuration files, application source code, etc.

- Attackers can manage to access files located outside the web root because of this vulnerability.

Example: http://www.example.com/abc.php=../../../../etc/passwd

Cross-site request forgery

Any request sent to the server are not validated (No server-side validation). The server processes the request without verifying whether the user made the request or not. Because of poor validation, requests can be forged and sent to users to force them to do things that they are not intended to do. By clicking some links, users may unknowingly change account passwords.

Command Injection

- Command injection vulnerability in a web application allows attackers to inject untrusted data and execute it as part of regular command or query.

- Attackers use specially crafted malicious commands or queries to exploit these vulnerabilities which may result in data loss.

- Injection attacks are possible because of poor web development capabilities.

File Inclusion

Local File Inclusion - Allows an attacker to gain access to any file on the server computer. An attacker can even access a file located apart from the web-root folder.

Remote File Inclusion - Allows an attacker to gain access to any file from any server. We can execute file located on a remote server on the vulnerable server.

SQL Injection:

SQL (Structured Query Language) is a database management language used to manage databases to perform various operations like create, read, update and delete on the database. SQL is used by database administrators, as well as developers to organize user data properly. Web applications interact with the database server in the form of queries. SQL queries include select, add, insert, update, delete, create, alter and truncate.

List of Database software

- MySQL
- Microsoft SQL
- Oracle
- MongoDB
- SQL lite
- Microsoft Access
- DB2 Express-C

Database

A database is a collection of information that is organized into rows, columns, and tables, and it is indexed so that it can be easily accessed, managed and updated. Data in the database gets updated, expanded and deleted as new information is added.

Relation between Web Server and Database Server

A server is a software that runs continuously and responds to requests sent by the clients, Communication between a client and a server happens using a specific protocol example HTTP, HTTPS Server running web application include three components like.

Web servers which primarily respond to HTTP / HTTPS requests sent by the clients and passes these requests on to handlers.

Application server handles requests to create dynamic web pages. The application server processes the user request to generate the HTML page for the end user, instead of serving a static HTML page stored on the disk. Application server software runs on the same physical server machine as where the web server is running.

Database Server is a server which houses a database application like JDBC, ODBC to provide database services to other computer programs. Most database applications respond to a query language. Each database understands its query language and converts each submitted query to server-readable form and executes it to retrieve results.

The relation between the web server and the database server are the web server uses the application server to retrieve the data from the database and host the data with the help of the web server application. So web server works as the front end, and database server works as a backend to provide data to web server.

SQL Injection

The technique used to take advantage of non-validated input vulnerabilities to pass SQL commands through a web application for execution on backend database to retrieve information directly from the database. It is used to gain unauthorized access to the database. SQL Injection is not a vulnerability in database or web server; it is vulnerability in a web application which occurs due to lack of input validation.

Types of SQL Injection attacks
- Authentication bypass attack
- Error-based SQL Injection
- Blind SQL Injection

Authentication bypass attack

The attacker uses this technique to bypass user authentication without providing the valid Username and password and tries to log into a web application with administrative privileges.

Authentication Bypass Cheat Sheet

1' or '1' = '1	admin' or 1=1
admin' --	admin' or 1=1--
admin' #	admin' or 1=1#
admin'/*	admin') or '1'='1'#
admin' or '1'='1	admin') or '1'='1'--
admin' or '1'='1'--	admin') or ('1'='1'/*
admin' or '1'='1'/*	admin') or ('1'='1'#
admin' or 1=1 or "="	admin') or ('1'='1'--
admin') or ('1'='1	admin' or ('1'='1
admin' or 1=1/*	admin' or 1=1#
or 1=1	or 1=1--
or 1=1#	or 1=1/*
admin' or 1=1 or "="	admin') or '1'='1/*

Error-based SQL Injection

Error-based SQL injection technique relies on error messages thrown by the database server to obtain information about the structure of the database. In some cases, error-based SQL injection alone is enough for an attacker to enumerate an entire database. While errors are very useful during the development phase of a web application, they should be disabled on a live site or logged to a file with restricted access instead. By analyzing these errors, the attacker can grab system information such as the database, database version, OS, etc.

Blind SQL injection

Blind SQL injection is a type of SQL Injection attack that queries the database true or false questions and determines the answer based on the applications response. This attack is often used when the web application is configured to show generic error messages but has not mitigated the code that is vulnerable to SQL injection. Blind SQL injection is nearly identical to normal SQL Injection, the only difference being the way the data is retrieved from the database.

Countermeasures for SQL Injection Vulnerabilties

- Never trust user input. Sanitize and validate all input fields. Use parameterized statements, separate data from SQL code.

- Reject entries that contain binary data, escape sequences and comment characters.

- Checking the privileges of a user's connection to the database.

- Use secure hash algorithms to secure user passwords stored in the database.

- Perform source code review before hosting website.

Countermeasures for other web application Vulnerabilities

- Define access rights to private folders on the web server.

- Validate user input length, perform bound checking

- Use language-specific libraries for the programming language.

- Use the more secure HTTPS protocol instead of HTTP if available.

- Log out from online user accounts instead of directly closing the browser, to properly end sessions.

- Take careful note of security warnings from the web browser

- Avoid clicking links to sensitive portals, such as for e-banking, instead enter the URL of the website manually.

- Keep web application building software (frameworks) up to date to protect websites from application-based attacks.

18
Hacking Mobile Platforms

Mobile operating system

A mobile operating system is an OS that is specifically designed to run on mobile devices such as mobile phones, smartphones, PDAs, tablet computers and other handheld devices. Mobile operating systems combine features of a personal computer operating system with other features useful for mobile or handheld use

List of Mobile OS

Android OS	Bada
BlackBerry OS	Palam OS
iPhone OS / iOS	WebOS
Windows Mobile	Symbian OS

Terms in Mobile Hacking

Stock ROM: It is the default ROM (Operating System) of an Android Device.

Rooting: Rooting is the process of allowing users of smartphones, tablets and other devices running the Android mobile operating system to attain privileged control (known as root access) over various Android subsystems.

Lineage OS: LineageOS is a free and open-source operating system for smartphones and tablet computers, based on the Android mobile platform. It is the successor to the custom ROM Cyanogen Mod

Bricking Mobile: A device that does not turn on and function normally. The bricked device cannot be fixed through normal procedures. Devices are bricked due to overwriting of the Firmware or low-level system software.

Bring Your Own Device (BYOD): Bring your own device (BYOD) is a business policy that allows employees to bring their mobile devices to their workplace.

Mobile Platform Vulnerabilities and Risks

- Malicious Apps in Store
- Mobile Malware
- Jailbreaking or Rooting
- Mobile Application Vulnerabilities
- Weak Data Security and App Encryption
- Excessive Permissions
- Weak Communication Security

Android OS

Android is a mobile operating system developed by Google, based on a modified version of the Linux kernel and other open source software and designed primarily for touchscreen mobile devices such as smartphones and tablets.

Android Architecture

Android Architecture is implemented in the form of a software stack architecture consisting of a Linux kernel, a runtime environment and corresponding libraries, an application framework and a set of applications.

iPhone OS (IOS)

iOS is a mobile operating system created and developed by Apple Inc. and distributed exclusively for Apple hardware. It is a proprietary operating system which runs on Apple mobile devices (iPhone, iPad, and iPod touch).

iOS Architecture

The architecture of iOS is a layered architecture. At the uppermost level iOS works as an intermediary between the underlying hardware and the applications running on the device. Apps communicate with the hardware through a collection of well-defined system interfaces instead of directly interacting with hardware.

Interfaces make it simple to write apps that constantly work on devices having various hardware abilities.

Hacking Android Device

Hacking Android By using Malicious App Infection

- Dendroid
- Droid Jack
- AndroRAT

Using Kernel Level Vulnerabilities to Exploit Mobile Devices

- Stage Fright

General Guidelines for Mobile Security

- Do not load too many applications and avoid auto-upload of photos to social networks.
- Securely wipe or delete the data disposing of the device.
- Turn of Bluetooth if it is not necessary.
- Do not share the information within GPS-enabled apps unless they are necessary.
- Install applications from trusted application stores.

Countermeasures

- Do not directly download Android Package Files from untrusted websites.
- Never root your Android device.
- Update the operating system regularly.
- Use iOS devices on a secured and protected WiFi network.
- Deploy only trusted third-party applications on iOS devices.
- Configure 'Find My iPhone' and utilize it to wipe a lost or stolen device.
- In the case of IT companies, it is important to educate employees in the organization about the BYOD policy.

19

Wireless Network Hacking (Wifi)

WiFi

- WiFi refers to wireless local area network (WLAN) works based on IEEE 802.11 standard. It is a widely used technology for wireless communication across a radio channel.

- Personal computers, smartphones, video game console, etc. use WiFi to connect to the internet via a wireless network access point.

- Every network card has a physical static address known as MAC address. This address is unique, and the card manufacturer assigns it.

- This address is used between devices to identify each other and to transfer packets to the right place. Each packet has a source MAC and a destination MAC.

WEP

Wired Equivalent Privacy (WEP) is a security algorithm for IEEE 802.11 wireless networks. Introduced as part of the original 802.11 standards ratified in 1997, its intention was to provide data confidentiality comparable to that of a traditional wired network. A Standard 64-bit WEP uses a 40-bit key (also known as WEP-40), which is concatenated with a 24-bit initialization vector (IV) to form the RC4 key used for encryption. RC4 is a stream cipher; the same traffic key must never be used twice. The purpose of an IV, which is transmitted as plain text, is to prevent any repetition, but a 24-bit IV is not long enough to ensure this on a busy network. The way the IV was used also opened WEP to a related key attack.

WPA

WPA stands for Wi-Fi Protected Access and is a security technology for Wi-Fi networks. It was developed in response to the weaknesses of WEP (Wired Equivalent Privacy) and therefore improves on WEP's authentication and encryption features.

WPA provides stronger encryption than WEP through use of either of two standard technologies: Temporal Key Integrity Protocol (TKIP) and Advanced Encryption Standard (AES). WPA also includes built-in authentication support that WEP does not offer. Some implementations of WPA allow for WEP clients to connect to the network too, but the security is then reduced to WEP-levels for all connected devices.

WPA includes support for authentication serves called Remote Authentication Dial-In User Service servers (RADIUS) servers. After connecting to a WPA network Once a device successfully connects to a WPA network. Devices make a four-way handshake with the access point to generate security keys.

When TKIP encryption is used, a message integrity code (MIC) is included to make sure that the data is not being spoofed. It replaces WEP's weaker packet guarantee called cyclic redundancy check (CRC).

WPA2

Short for Wi-Fi Protected Access 2, WPA2 is the security method added to WPA for wireless networks that provide stronger data protection and network access control. It provides enterprise and consumer Wi-Fi users with a high level of assurance that only authorized users can access their wireless networks. Based on the IEEE 802.11i standard, WPA2 provides government grade security by implementing the National Institute of Standards and Technology (NIST) FIPS 140-2 compliant AES encryption algorithm and 802.1x-based authentication.

There are two versions of WPA2: WPA2-Personal, and WPA2- Enterprise. WPA2-Personal protects unauthorized network access by utilizing a set-up password. WPA2-Enterprise verifies network users through a server. WPA2 is backward compatible with WPA.

WPA3

WPA3 is the next generation of Wi-Fi security and provides cutting-edge security protocols to the market. Building on the widespread success and adoption of Wi-Fi CERTIFIED WPA2™, WPA3 adds new features to simplify Wi-Fi security, enable more robust authentication, deliver increased cryptographic strength for highly sensitive data markets, and maintain resiliency of mission-critical networks. All WPA3 networks

- Use the latest security methods
- Disallow outdated legacy protocols

- Require use of Protected Management Frames (PMF)

Since Wi-Fi networks differ in usage purpose and security needs, WPA3 includes additional capabilities specifically for personal and enterprise networks. Users of WPA3-Personal receive increased protection from password guessing attempts, while WPA3-Enterprise users can now take advantage of higher grade security protocols for sensitive data networks.

WPA3 which retains interoperability with WPA2™ devices is currently an optional certification for Wi-Fi CERTIFIED devices. It will become required over time as market adoption grows.

WPA3-Personal

WPA3-Personal brings better protections to individual users by providing more robust password-based authentication, even when users choose passwords that fall short of typical complexity recommendations. This capability is enabled through Simultaneous Authentication of Equals (SAE), which replaces Pre-shared Key (PSK) and WPA2-Personal. The technology is resistant to offline dictionary attacks where an adversary attempts to determine a network password by trying possible passwords without further network interaction.

- Natural password selection: Allows users to choose passwords that are easier to remember

- Ease of use: Delivers enhanced protections with no change to the way users connect to a network

- Forward secrecy: Protects data traffic even if a password is compromised after the data was transmitted

WPA3-Enterprise

WPA3-Enterprise. WPA3-Enterprise builds upon WPA2 and ensures the Enterprise, governments, and financial institutions have greater security with consistent application of security protocols across the network.

WPA3-Enterprise also offers an optional mode using 192-bit minimum-strength security protocols and cryptographic tools to better protect sensitive data:

- Authenticated encryption: 256-bit Galois/Counter Mode Protocol (GCMP-256)

- Key derivation and confirmation: 384-bit Hashed Message Authentication Mode (HMAC) with Secure Hash Algorithm (HMAC- SHA384)

- Key establishment and authentication: Elliptic Curve Diffie-Hellman (ECDH) exchange and Elliptic Curve Digital Signature Algorithm (ECDSA) using a 384- bit elliptic curve

- Robust management frame protection: 256-bit Broadcast/Multicast Integrity Protocol Galois Message Authentication Code (BIP-GMAC- 256)

The 192-bit security mode offered by WPA3-Enterprise ensures the right combination of cryptographic tools are used and sets a consistent baseline of security within a WPA3 network.

Types of Wireless Antennas

Directional Antenna: is used to broadcast and obtain radio waves from a single direction.

Omnidirectional Antenna: provides a 360-degree horizontal radiation pattern. It is used in wireless base stations.

Parabolic Grid Antenna is based on the principle of a satellite dish, but it does not have a solid backing. They can pick up WiFi signals ten miles or more.

Yagi Antenna is a unidirectional antenna commonly used in communications for a frequency band of 10 MHz to VHF and UHF.

Dipole Antenna is a bidirectional antenna, used to support client connections rather than site-to-site applications.

Finding Open WiFi Networks
War Walking - Attackers walk around with WiFi-enabled laptops to detect open wireless networks.

War Chalking - A method used to draw symbols in public places to advertise open WiFi networks.

War Flying - In this technique, attackers use drones to detect open wireless networks.

War Driving - Attackers drive around with WiFi-enabled laptops to detect open wireless networks.

Aircrack-ng

Aircrack-ng includes a set of tools to perform WiFi network hacking.

Monitoring: Packet capture and export of data to text files for further processing by third-party tools.

Attacking: Replay attacks, deauthentication, fake access points and others via packet injection.

Testing: Checking WiFi cards and driver capabilities (capture and injection).

Cracking: WEP and WPA PSK (WPA 1 and 2).

Airmon-ng

This script can be used to enable monitor mode on wireless interfaces. It may also be used to go back from monitor mode to managed mode. Entering the airmon-ng command without parameters will show the interfaces status.

Airodump-ng

Airodump-ng is used for packet capturing of raw 802.11 frames and is particularly suitable for collecting WEP IVs (Initialization Vector) for the intent of using them with aircrack-ng. If you have a GPS receiver connected to the computer, airodump-ng is capable of logging the coordinates of the found access points.

Additionally, airodump-ng writes out several files containing the details of all access points and clients seen.

Terminology:

Bssid	=	Mac Address of the Access Point
Essid	=	Name of the Access Point
Ch	=	Channel Number of Access Point
Data	=	Data Packets Transferred
Beacons	=	Avertisement Packets Sent by Access Point
Pwr	=	Signal Strength of Access Point
Auth	=	Encryption Used by the Access Point

| Cipher | = | Encryption Cipher Used by the Access Point |

Aireplay-ng

Aireplay-ng is used to inject frames. The primary function is to generate traffic for the later use in aircrack-ng for cracking the WEP and WPA-PSK keys. There are different attacks which can cause de-authentications to capture WPA handshake data, fake authentications, Interactive packet replay, hand-crafted ARP request injection and ARP-request reinjection. With the packet forge-ng tool, it's possible to create arbitrary frames. Most drivers need to be patched to be able to inject,

Airbase-ng

Airbase-ng is a multi-purpose tool aimed at attacking clients as opposed to the Access Point (AP) itself. Since it is so versatile and flexible, summarizing it is a challenge. Here are some of the feature highlights:

- Implements the Caffe Latte WEP client attack
- Implements the Hirte WEP client attack
- Ability to cause the WPA/WPA2 handshake to be captured
- Ability to act as an ad-hoc Access Point
- Ability to serve as a full Access Point
- Ability to filter by SSID or client MAC addresses
- Ability to manipulate and resend packets
- Ability to encrypt sent packets and decrypt received packets

WEP Cracking

It uses a stream cipher algorithm called RC4 where each packet is encrypted at the AP and is then decrypted at the client, WEP ensures that each packet has a unique keystream by using a random 24-bit Initialization Vector (IV), this IV is contained in the packets as plain text.

In a busy network we can collect more than two packets with the same IV, then we can use the aircrack-ng suite to determine WEP key.

Cracking WPA/WPA2 Encryption

Capturing WPA packets is not useful as they do not contain any info that can be used to crack the key. The only packet that contains info that helps us crack the password is the handshake packets.

Every time a client connects to that AP a four-way handshake occurs between the client and the AP. By capturing the handshake, we can use aircrack to launch a word list attack against the handshake to determine the key.

To crack a WPA/WPA2 AP with WPS disabled, we need two things:

1. Capture the Handshake
2. A wordlist

Cracking the WPA Key using a wordlist

Use aircrack-ng to crack the key. It performs the job by combining each password in the wordlist with AP names (Essid) to compute a PMK (Pairwise Master Key) using the pbkdf2 algorithm; the PMK is then compared to the handshake file. Create wordlist using crunch tool to crack the WPA key

Exploiting WPS Feature

WPS is a feature that allows users to connect to WPS enabled networks easily, using a WPS button or only by clicking on WPS functionality. Authentication is done using an eight-digit long pin, this means that there is a relatively small number of pin combination and using brute force we can guess the pin in less than 10 hours. Tools like wifite or reaver can automate this process and recover the WPA key from that pin.

Note: This flaw is in the WPS feature and not in WPA/WPA2. However, it allows us to crack any WPA/WPA2 AP without using a wordlist and without any clients.

Countermeasures:
- Do not use WEP encryption, as it is easy to crack.
- Use WPA2 with a complex password, make sure the password contains small letters, capital letters, symbols and numbers

Thirumalesh

- Ensure that the WPS feature is disabled as it can be used to crack your complex WPA2 key by brute-forcing the easy WPS pin.
- Enable MAC address filtering on access point or router.
- Set default router access password and enable firewall protection.

The Complete Ethical Hacking Book

20

Cloud Computing

Cloud Computing

Cloud Computing is the practice of using a network of remote servers hosted on the internet to store, manage, and process data, rather than a local server or a personal computer. The information being accessed is found in "the cloud" so the user need not to be in a specific place to gain access in which data is stored.

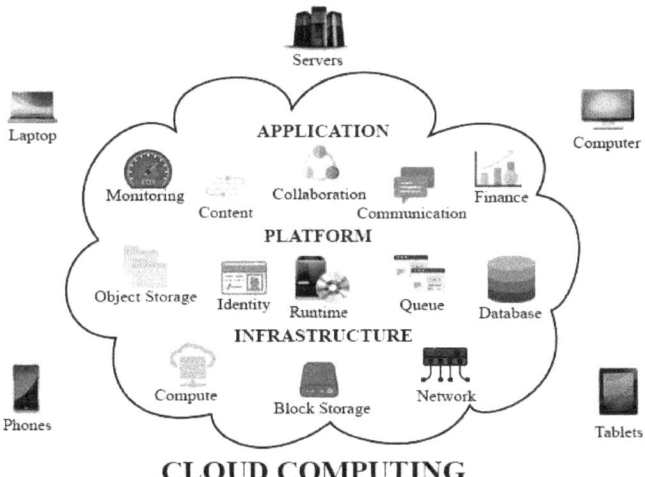

Characteristics of cloud computing

- On-demand self-service
- Distributed storage
- Rapid elasticity
- Automated management
- Broad network access

- Resource pooling
- Measured service
- Virtualization technology
- Pay per use

Cloud Computing Services

1. Infrastructure as a Service (IaaS)
2. Platform as a service (PaaS)
3. Software as a service (SaaS)

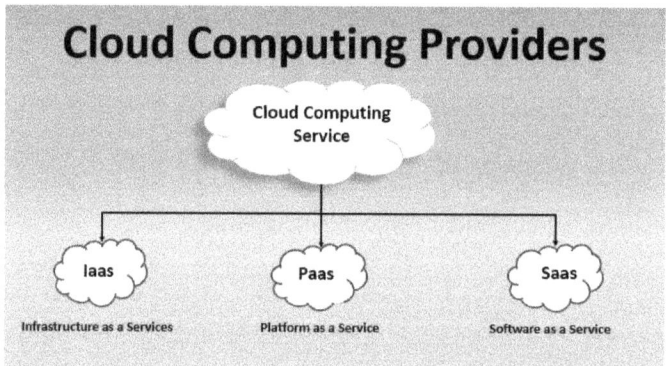

Infrastructure as a Service (IaaS)

Infrastructure-as-a-Service (IaaS) provides virtual machines and other abstracted hardware and operating systems which may be controlled through service API. In these services, cloud service providers install operating system images, and application software's on the cloud infrastructure based on user's requirement. The cloud service provider is responsible for patching and maintains the operating systems and the application software.

Examples: Amazon EC2, SkyDrive, etc.

Platform-as-a-Service (PaaS)

Platform-as-a-Service (PaaS) offers development tools, configuration management, and development platforms on-demand that can be used by subscribers to develop custom applications; typically it includes a framework that satisfies the requirement of a developer. The Application developers can take advantage of using the licensed software without worrying about the cost and complexity involved in maintaining the underlying hardware and software layers.

Examples: Google App Engine, Microsoft Azure, etc.

Software as a Service (SaaS)

Software-as-a-Service (SaaS) offers software to subscribers on-demand over the Internet. CSP (Cloud service provider) manages the infrastructure and platforms that run these applications. This service eliminates the need for installing and running the applications on the user's computers.

Examples: Google Docs, Calendar, Web-based office applications, etc.

Cloud deployment models:

Public Cloud	Community Cloud
Private cloud	Hybrid Cloud

Public cloud

In the public cloud model, The cloud service provider delivers the cloud service over the internet to users. Where users no need to worry about the infrastructure. The cost is shared by all users, for free or in the form of a license policy like pay per user.

Private Cloud

Private Cloud infrastructure is operated solely by a single organization. The services are delivered from an organizational data center to internal users of the organization. This model preserves the management, control, and security to organizational data centers. Internal users may not be billed for services. Private clouds are great for organizations that have high-security demands, high management demands and uptime requirements.

Community cloud

Community Cloud infrastructure is mutually shared between organizations that belong to a specific community with common concerns (security, compliance, etc.). The community members generally share similar privacy, performance and security concerns. A community cloud can be managed by hosting it internally or by a third- party provider. A community cloud is good for organizations that work on joint ventures that need centralized cloud computing ability for managing, building and executing their projects. The best example for community cloud is a cloud for the bank or trading firm.

Hybrid Cloud

Hybrid cloud computing uses a combination of two or more cloud deployment models, like private cloud and public cloud services. This service allows workloads to be shared between private and public clouds. Companies can run mission-critical workloads or sensitive applications on the private cloud and use the public cloud to handle workload bursts or spikes in demand. An organization can use the public cloud to interact with their customers while keeping their data secured through a private cloud.

Cloud Computing Benefits:

Security

- Less investment in security
- Better disaster recovery
- Effective patch management and implementation of security updates

Economic

- Environment-friendly
- Less maintenance
- Less Power consumption

Operational

- Deploy applications quickly
- Scale as needed

Staffing

- Less IT staff
- Well usage of resources
- Less personnel training

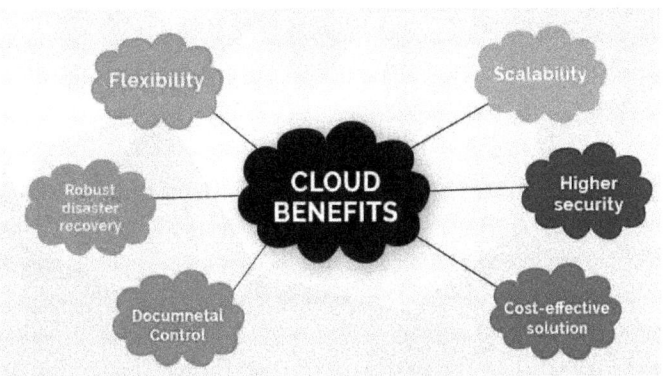

Cloud Computing Threats

- Illegal access to the Cloud
- Privilege Escalation.
- Hardware Failure.
- VM-Level attacks.
- Cryptanalysis Attacks.
- SQL Injection Attacks.
- DoS and DDoS Attacks.
- Session Hijacking using XSS Attacks.
- Loss of Business Reputation due to Co-tenant Activity

Cloud Security Tools:

Applications	Web App Firewalls, Scanners, Transactional Security
Information	Strong Encryption, Database Activity Monitoring, DLP
Management	Patch Management, Configuration Management
Network	NIDS/NIPS, Firewalls, Deep Packet Inspection, Anti-DDoS
Trusted Computing	Hardware & Software API's

Computer and Storage	Host-based Firewall, HIDS/HIPS, Integrity & File/Log Management
Physical	Physical Plant Security, CCTV, Guards

Countermeasures:

- Enforce data protection, backup and retention mechanisms.
- Disclose relevant logs and data to customers.
- Prevent unauthorized server access using security checkpoint.
- Monitor the client's traffic for any malicious activity.
- Implement strong key generation, stronger authentication management, and destruction practices.
- Check for data protection at both design and runtime.
- Enforce legal contracts in employee behavior policy.
- Prohibit users from sharing application and services credentials.
- Ensure that physical security is a 24 x 7
- Leverage strong two-factor authentication techniques where possible.

21

Cryptography

Cryptography

Cryptography is a process of converting plain text data (readable) into ciphertext (unreadable) data to protect confidentiality so that unauthorized users cannot understand what is transmitted. Encryption algorithms are used to perform mathematical computation on data using the key and convert data to ciphertext. The algorithm that is chosen to perform encryption with some key can also be used for decryption. Decryption is the process of converting ciphertext to plaintext. Encryption is a reversible operation, i.e., converting plaintext to ciphertext and vice versa is possible using the algorithm and key. Cryptography is used to protect the confidentiality of information shared on the internet such as email messages, chat sessions, web transactions, personal data, corporate data, e-commerce applications, etc.

Cryptography method of Encryption

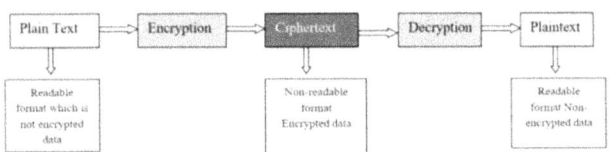

Objectives of Cryptography

Confidentiality: To ensure that private or confidential information is not made available or disclosed to unauthorized individuals.

Integrity: To ensure that an unauthorized individual does not tamper the information exchanged over the internet.

Availability: To ensure that services are not denied to authorized users.

Types of Cryptography

Based on the number of keys used for encryption they are classified into two types

- Symmetric key cryptography
- Asymmetric key cryptography

Symmetric Encryption

The symmetric key algorithm is also known as the secret key algorithm. Symmetric key algorithms use the same cryptographic key for both encryption and decryption. Data Encryption Standard (DES) and Advanced Encryption Standard (AES) algorithms are the most commonly used symmetric key algorithm which uses a key at sender side for encryption, and the receiver uses the same key for decryption. To make two parties (sender and receiver) to communicate confidentially, they must first exchange the secret key so that each party can encrypt messages to send and decrypt messages to read. This process is known as key exchange. This key is shared between two parties over a secure channel. Based on input data these algorithms can be further divided into two categories

Block ciphers: Block ciphers encrypt data one block at a time.

Stream ciphers: Stream ciphers encrypt data byte by byte.

The strength of any cryptographic algorithm depends on the secrecy of the key. If keys are not securely shared, then unauthorized parties can gain access to a secret key used for encryption and they can un-encrypt data and read every packet shared between two parties.

Symmetric Encryption

Asymmetric Encryption

Asymmetric key algorithms use two different keys known as a public key and a private key for encryption and decryption. The sender and receiver generate a private key which is kept secret (not shared with anyone) and a public key which is shared with other parties. In case of asymmetric algorithms, senders encrypt messages using the receiver's public key. The receiver's private key can only decrypt this encrypted message. In this manner, it ensures that both the confidentiality and integrity of information are preserved. The best part of asymmetric encryption is its Key Management system; it takes advantage of Public Key Infrastructure for proper management of public keys.

Cipher

In cryptography, a cipher is an algorithm that performs encryption or decryption in a series of well-defined steps that can be followed as a procedure. Ciphers are classified based on input data, a number of keys used for encryption.

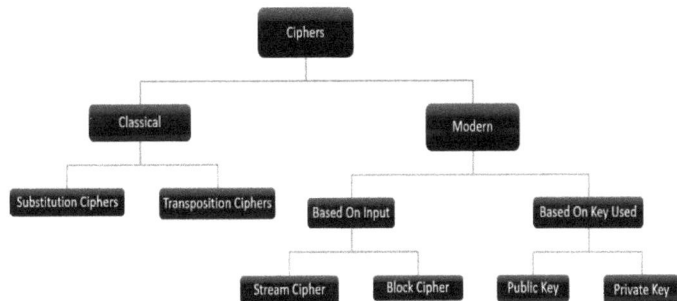

Classical ciphers

Classical ciphers are cryptographic algorithms that have been used in the past (practically computed and solved manually). Classical ciphers are often divided into substitution ciphers and transposition ciphers.

Substitution cipher: In a substitution cipher, letters are systematically replaced throughout the message for other letters. In these cipher method monoalphabetic substitution ciphers, where just one cipher alphabet is used. Polyalphabetic substitution cipher, where multiple cipher alphabets are used.

Transposition ciphers: In a transposition cipher, the letters themselves are kept unchanged, but their order within the message is scrambled. Many transposition ciphers are done according to geometric design.

Modern ciphers

Modern ciphers are designed based on various concepts of mathematics such as number theory, computational complexity theory, and probability theory. It needs the computational power to encrypt and decrypt the data. Modern encryption methods are divided into two type based on input data (Block and Stream ciphers), and a number of keys (secret key and public key) used.

Hash function

A hash function performs a series of mathematical operations to convert input data into a fixed length alphanumeric characters. The input to the hash function is an arbitrary length, but the output is always of fixed length.

Features of Hash Functions

- Fixed Length Output: Hash function converts data of arbitrary length to a fixed length.

- The efficiency of Operation: Computationally hash functions are much faster than asymmetric encryption.

Examples of the Hash functions

These are examples of well-known hash functions:

Hashed Message Authentication Code (HMAC): Combines authentication via a shared secret with hashing.

Message Digest 2 (MD2): Byte-oriented, produces a 128-bit hash value from an arbitrary-length message, designed for smart cards.

MD4: Similar to MD2, designed specifically for fast processing in software.

MD5: Similar to MD4 but slower because the data is manipulated more.

Secure Hash Algorithm (SHA): Modeled after MD4 and proposed by NIST for the.

Secure Hash Standard (SHS), produces a 160-bit hash value.

Steganography

Steganography is an art of hiding a secret message within an ordinary message and extracting it at the destination to maintain the confidentiality of data. The program named 'snow' is used to conceal messages in ASCII text by appending whitespace to the end of lines. There are different tools that can hide text in pictures so that to retrieve the hidden secret message the receiver must use the same tool as sender used to hide the text message. Steganalysis is the art of discovering and rendering secret messages using steganography.

Cryptography Attacks

Cryptography attacks are based on the assumption that the cryptanalyst has access to the encrypted information.

- Chosen plaintext
- Adaptive chosen plaintext attack
- Known plaintext
- Known ciphertext
- Chosen ciphertext
- Chosen key
- Rubber cosh cryptanalysis

Brute force attack is a process of defeating a cryptographic scheme by trying a large number of possible keys until the correct encryption key is discovered.

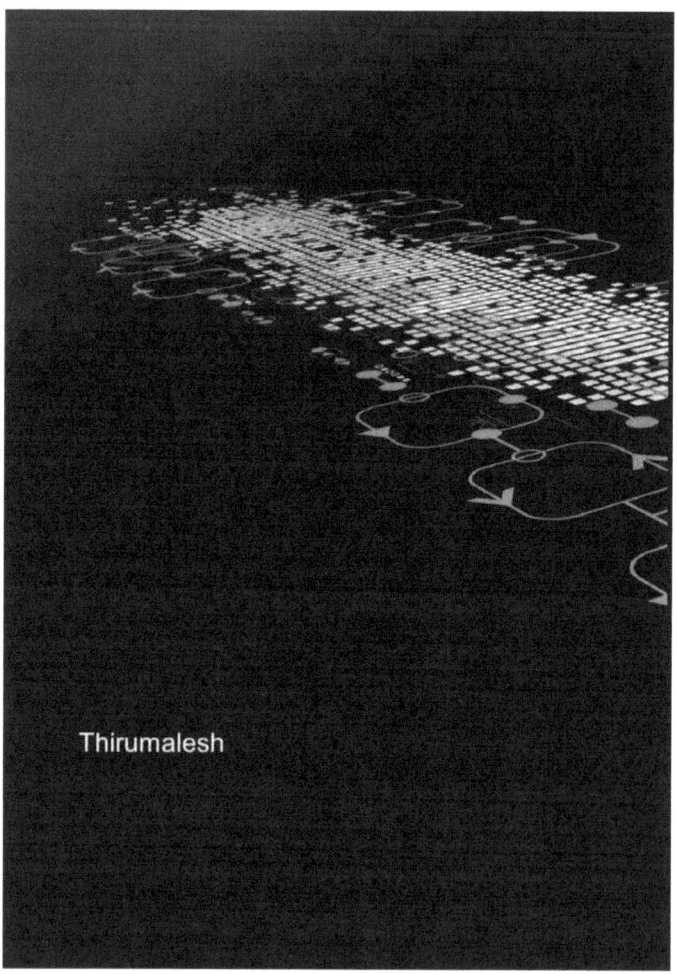

www.ingramcontent.com/pod-product-compliance
Lightning Source LLC
LaVergne TN
LVHW070522070526
838199LV00072B/6679